START

it

UP

First published in 2011 by
Zest Books, an imprint of Orange Avenue Publishing
35 Stillman Street, Suite 121, San Francisco, CA 94107
www.zestbooks.net
Created and produced by Zest Books, San Francisco, CA

© 2011 by Orange Avenue Publishing LLC

Typeset in PMN Caecilia and Beton EF; Title text set in Aachen Bold
Teen Nonfiction / Business & Economics

Library of Congress Control Number: 2010936580

ISBN-13: 978-0-9819733-5-7
ISBN-10: 0-9819733-5-3

CREDITS
EDITORIAL DIRECTOR/BOOK EDITOR: Karen Macklin
CREATIVE DIRECTOR: Hallie Warshaw
ART DIRECTOR: Tanya Napier
GRAPHIC DESIGNER: Marissa Fiend
ILLUSTRATORS: Eriko Takada and Marissa Fiend
RESEARCH EDITOR: Nikki Roddy
MANAGING and PRODUCTION EDITOR: Pam McElroy

ADVISORS
BUSINESS ADVISOR: Ryan T. Wright M.B.A., Ph.D., Assistant Professor in Business and Entrepreneurship at University of San Francisco
TEEN ADVISORS: Emma Herlihy, Celina Reynes, Diana Rae Valenzuela, Irene Xu

Manufactured in China
LEO 10 9 8 7 6 5 4 3 2 1
4500268869

START it UP

The **COMPLETE TEEN BUSINESS GUIDE** to Turning Your Passions Into Pay

By Kenrya Rankin

Foreword

by Chris Gorog
founder and CEO of HeadlineShirts.com

I BECAME AN ENTREPRENEUR as soon as I was big enough to hold a snow shovel. I was eight, and I went around to all of our older neighbors and offered to shovel their walks for $10 each time if they would hire me as their snow shoveler for the season. If they only wanted to hire me job by job, it would cost $20 each time. After the first snowfall I signed up 10 houses. It snows a lot in Princeton, New Jersey, so I was doing pretty well for a fourth grader.

By high school, I was mowing lawns and building computers. Then one night, I went to a Green Day concert and saw a great opportunity. The first 500 people to enter the concert had received wristbands, which gave them ground floor (mosh pit) access. But many of the early arrivals were younger kids with their parents, and the parents wanted to get rid of the wristbands so that their kids wouldn't get roughed up in the mosh pit. I bought the wristbands from the parents, then sold them for three times the cost an hour later to the teens who really wanted them, but hadn't arrived early enough to get them.

These ventures might seem small, but they were significant. With each one, I recognized a new customer need and came up with a way to fulfill it. Then in 2004, I founded my current business, HeadlineShirts.com, a leading internet T-shirt company and top supplier to Urban Outfitters. I love my company, and I believe we have been successful because our T-shirts are a little smarter, a little better made, and a little more environmentally sustainable than others in the market.

But starting my business wasn't easy. From raising capital to structuring the company to finding my market, there was always a lot to think about. And I made a lot of mistakes on my way to where I am now. For example, I tried to expand too quickly—making things like button down shirts, jackets, and ties, at a time when the economy was contracting—and almost went out of business as a result. The company bounced back, but the experience was painful. Mistakes are important for the things they teach us. But not all mistakes are necessary. And many of my mistakes might have been avoided if I'd had the hands-on guidance of this book.

Start It Up is a great tool for entrepreneurs. The author, business journalist Kenrya Rankin, covers a wide range of topics related to starting a business, from figuring out what kind of company you want to run, picking out a name to filing all of your paperwork, coming up with price points, deciding who to hire and learning how to use your business to help the world. Throughout the book, successful young entrepreneurs offer their advice and personal stories. Plus, this book is truly fun to read.

Every entrepreneur has a few secret weapons that helped turn their dreams into reality. This book should be one of yours!

Table of Contents

1

ENTREPRENEURIAL YOU
Passion Isn't Just for Your Dating Life   page 8

2

WHO'S GOT YOUR BACK?
Establishing a Support System   page 26

3

GETTING SERIOUS
Creating a Business Plan   page 38

4

THE TECHNICAL STUFF
Making Your Business Official   page 52

5

MONEY MATTERS
How to Amass and Protect Your Fortune   page 64

6

WHO'S THE BOSS?
How to Hire and Manage Your Crew page 82

7

EXTRA, EXTRA
Telling the World About Your Big Idea page 98

8

REPEAT BUSINESS
Customer Service Rules page 112

9

DOING GOOD
Using Your Business to Improve the World page 122

10

NOW WHAT?
To Grow or Let It Go page 138

CHAPTER 1

ENTREPRENEURIAL YOU

Passion Isn't Just for Your Dating Life

If you're like most teenagers, you're being pulled in a million directions. Between keeping up your grades, joining clubs to make your college apps look good, and holding down a job so you can actually afford to do the fun stuff, it can be a bit much. But what if you could combine a couple of those things and make money by doing what makes you happy? And even better, never again have to work at a clothing store at the mall or while away the hours serving fries at the fast food spot on the corner. What if, instead, you could design your own brilliant fall line of clothing and sell it to your classmates? Or bake your world-famous chocolate chip cookies for a profit instead of giving them to your freeloading friends for nothing? Turns out you can—by becoming an entrepreneur.

What Is an Entrepreneur?

An entrepreneur is basically someone who comes up with a great idea for a business and then makes it happen. The recipe is simple:

1. Find something you love to do.
2. Figure out how to make money on it.
3. Work hard to pull it off.

There's no better time than the present to start your own business. And the best part is that the skills you'll learn from running your own company could keep you from ever having to work a 9 to 5.

Starting a business means taking notes—lots of them. So as you read, have a notebook or computer nearby. Every time you see this icon , you need to take some notes or do some brainstorming. The info you jot down is essential to shaping your vision and helping you to create a business plan (more about that in Chapter 3).

Are You an Entrepreneur?

First thing's first: Do you have what it takes to run your own business? There are as many different types of entrepreneurs as there are companies, and part of the fun of doing your own thing is figuring out what methods work best for you. Listed here are ten traits that many successful entrepreneurs share. The more of them you possess, the easier things will be in the beginning.

> Don't think that just because you're young, you can't be an entrepreneur. A lot of kids are like, "You can't start a business when you're 13," but you can! There's nothing that says an entrepreneur has to be a certain age. If you want to do something great and be a young business professional, go for it.
>
> —Gabrielle McBay, founded cookie company Crumbs by Gabrielle at age 13

If you're short on these qualities but still want to have your own business, know that owning a business can actually *teach* you some of these things.

❶ You have a passion. Whether it's making your own jewelry, cutting hair, playing video games, working on old cars, or something else completely, there's at least one thing you love to do in your free time. The most successful entrepreneurs find a way to do what they love for cash so they actually enjoy their work.

❷ You're not afraid of hard work. Yeah, it might suck a little, but you know that if you dig in, you can accomplish any task, whether it's banging out an essay for English class or getting up at 5 am each and every day for swim team practice. The ability to work hard will help you handle all the difficult things that can come with starting a company.

❸ You have an independent spirit. While you probably work well in groups, you also thrive when working alone. No matter how many people eventually join your staff, there will be plenty of things that you have to handle yourself, which might mean spending late nights designing websites in your room after you finish your homework. But that's cool because you enjoy the feeling of completing a task on your own.

❹ You're good at planning. You are excellent at setting goals and figuring out the steps you need to take to get there. At school, you know that turning in an A+ paper means picking a topic, researching it, writing it, and proofreading it. So you start two weeks before the due date and put yourself on a step-by-step schedule to get it all done in time. You'll use this skill to plan all the specifics of your company.

❺ You manage money well. You're not rich by any stretch, but you do know how to stretch a dollar. When you get $50 in a birthday card, you spend half and save the rest, rather than blowing it all on video games and who knows what. Plus, you know how to get the most for each buck you *do* decide to spend, so you'll be great at handling your company's finances and reinvesting in your business.

❻ You're a good communicator. You enjoy (at least somewhat) talking to other people—in person, on the phone, or online—and you're pretty good at getting your point across in writing, too.

Running a company means maintaining open lines of communication with people, whether it's with your employees and clients or potential customers and investors, so it's important that you feel comfortable doing that.

7 You multitask with ease. If juggling a million things effortlessly were an Olympic sport, you'd win the gold. Meet with your chemistry study group? OK. Load the dishwasher? No problem. Talk your friend through a family crisis? You're all over it. You can do it all and do it all well. And that's a good thing because running a business means that you'll have a lot of things to manage each day.

8 You can ask for help. While you're quite capable of making things happen on your own, you're good at recognizing when you need to bring in the reinforcements, and you're not afraid to raise your hand for assistance. Being able to lean on your parents and friends will help you get around the barriers that will inevitably pop up on your road to success.

9 You're not too modest. You know how to talk up yourself and your pursuits when the time is right. That doesn't mean you're an arrogant jerk—that won't get you anywhere. But whether it's in a scholarship essay or on a phone

> *It's important to be fearless. Everyone calls our generation lazy and a little bit crazy, but you know what? Young people are doing amazing things each day, whether it's building the next hot technology start-up or saving the world by raising thousands of dollars for charity.*
>
> *— Crystal Yan, founded book project* What's Next: 25 Big Ideas from Gen-Yers Under 25 *at age 17*

call with your rich aunt, you can speak up about what makes you amazing when it counts most. This quality will help you tell prospective investors and clients why they need to give you their money and would-be staffers why they should work for you. No one will know just how great your product or service is if you don't tell them.

10 **You know how to take charge.** You don't automatically have to be in charge of every group project at school or run your crew of friends, but if you're put at the helm of something, you have the uncanny ability to take the lead and bring people together. You rock at inspiring others to work toward a common goal, and that will be key in gathering support for your company and managing a staff, should you choose to hire one.

What's Your Goal?

People have different reasons for starting businesses. What's yours? Figuring out exactly why you want to start your own business will go a long way toward making it happen. Do you want to earn enough money to pay for college? Just want to clear enough cash to finance your video game habit? Or are your goals more career oriented? Perhaps you hope to get experience rebuilding computer systems so you can work for a major tech company as an adult or you think that starting a photography business now, even if you don't make big bucks, will help you secure a great gig down the line. Or maybe you need a creative outlet to channel all the thoughts bouncing around in your head or you see a need that you can fill.

High school friends Josh Abramson and Ricky Van Veen created CollegeHumor .com in 1999 because they wanted an easy way to keep track of all the funny pictures and videos their friends were sending each other while everyone was away at college. Their site became one of the top comedy websites on the internet, and they went on to launch two MTV shows and various other related businesses. Pull out your notebook 📔 and brainstorm all the things you'd like to gain from running your own company. Later on, in chapters 6 and 9, you'll revisit these notes to see if you're on track.

What's in It for You?

Running your own business—as opposed to working for someone else—can be challenging, but it has amazing rewards. Here is a short list.

* **More independence.** Running a business is really about running your life. Most teenagers spend a good portion of their time being told what to do by everyone they know—parents, teachers, coaches—but when you run your own business, you're the boss. You set your hours, you call the shots.

* **More money.** Who doesn't want more cash? When you have your own business, you have the potential to make more money than at a minimum wage job because you price your product and you decide how many hours you want to work. So you can take on as many clients as you can fit around all your other stuff to make the extra cash to, say, download a ton of music.

* **More fun.** Rather than suffering through abuse from the shin-kickers at the shoe store and coming home smelling like synthetic leather, you

The Tip Jar TIPS

Make Some Time

Any entrepreneur will tell you that finding the time to do everything is one of the hardest things about running a company. It's really important to get your schedule under control now, before things get busy with your business. Most of us can free up time in our day by asking ourselves some tough questions: "Do I really need to talk to my best friend for two hours *every* night?" "Will the world end if I see only one movie on Saturday?" "And just how many minutes *do* I spend taking online quizzes and adding pictures to my profile pages?" Cut back on some of the less necessary things now, and you'll free up valuable time that you'll need to run your business later.

can make money doing what you actually enjoy. Why waste time doing something you hate just to bring home a paycheck?

* **More experience.** Owning a business is an amazing way to prepare for your future. For instance, cutting your friends' hair after school will get you ready to run your own salon. And even if you decide to do something completely different after college, the skills that you develop while managing a company—project supervision, marketing, dealing with finances—will help you succeed in any field.

What Will Make It Tough

Of course, having your own business isn't all fun and games. It does come with some obstacles, especially for young people. Here are a few of them.

* **It can be hard to find the time to get it started.** You're probably already super busy. Starting and running a business takes no small amount of time. You'll have to adjust your schedule to make it work. But hey! If you can squeeze in 15 hours slinging smoothies at the mall every week, you can use that time to work on your own stuff.

* **You might need help.** Sometimes you might have to go to the adults in your life and ask them to help you open a bank account, loan you money, or assist you with legal documents that you can't file unless you're over 18. It might be a little annoying that you can't do it all on your own, but asking for help is

I would have to say that the hardest thing for me is managing everything. We're in a lot of different cities, and I have a director and three instructors—and tons of homework.

—Amiya Alexander, founded Amiya's Mobile
Dance Academy at age 10

also a great way to get your parents involved in your life (or at least that's what you should tell them when you're pleading for a fifty).

❋ **Old people don't always trust young people.** Because of your age, there is always going to be someone who doesn't take you as seriously as he should. It's not a reflection of your skill or ability; it just means you have to work a little harder to get some people to patronize your business. And if there are adults— or even people your own age—who refuse to do business with you, forget about them. There are other potential customers out there just waiting to give you their money. Concentrate on building your product, and the people who were initially down on you may even come around.

❋ **You could be broke for a little while.** While you'll get a paycheck after flipping burgers for a week or two, it could take months before you see a profit from your business grilling burgers for outdoor events. Hopefully, your parents will be so proud of you for taking initiative that they'll help you out until you start raking it in. If not, make sure to save up some money before taking the plunge.

Figuring Out Your Biz

As you consider what kind of business you want to start, you should first ask yourself: "How can I get people to pay me to do the things I love to do?" The best way to figure that out is to identify those things. Start now by writing down 📄 all of the things you are passionate about.

Now look at your list. Which of those things do people really need? You may need to be creative in your thinking. For instance, you might be the fastest texter around, but that's not going to make you any money. However, you might be able to work as a freelance blogger or a typist. And while you'll never get paid for petting the dogs at the park, you can totally start a business walking them for your busy neighbors. Now go back to your list and, next to each passion, jot down an idea or two of how it might make you money. As long as you can see someone digging crumpled dollar bills out of their jeans and handing them over, you're on the right track.

How I Started My Business

I was shopping with my mom and saw a really cool T-shirt with the OmniPeace logo on it. There was a description of the company on the tag, and it said that OmniPeace donates 25 percent of its profits to humanitarian efforts to promote peace, education, human rights, and the eradiction of poverty in Africa by 2025. I was inspired by what this company was doing and wanted to be a part of it, so I had a crazy idea that I could make jewelry for them. I wrote a letter describing my idea and explaining how I really wanted to help them accomplish their goal. Four months later I received an email saying they loved my idea! From that day on, I've been working on my business. Over the next year, I designed my bracelets, found a factory that could make them, finalized numerous contracts with OmniPeace, and came up with a price for my product. It's been hard, but my dream has become my reality.

—Alexa Carlin, founded OmniPeace
   jewelry line Alexa Rose at age 17

Quiz! Finding Your Niche

Already got an idea for the company you want to start? Great! If you need a little help figuring out what type of business is right for you, take this quiz.

1. **It's time to join a homecoming committee. You pick:**

   a. Decorations. You can't wait to turn the gym into a winter wonderland!

   b. Cleanup. You like to put stuff back in order.

   c. Entertainment. You can make the school's sound system sound like Madison Square Garden's.

   d. Setup. You can build the platform for the homecoming court with your eyes closed.

2. **It's Saturday, and you finally have time to hang out. You:**

   a. Grab your camera and hit the park to look for something Facebook worthy.

   b. Help your friend plan a killer date for later that night.

   c. Set up the new HDTV you picked out for your family.

   d. Go to the gym and lift weights, enjoying the burn.

3. **Your dad is yelling for your help. He wants you to:**

   a. Pick out a tie to go with his outfit; you always know which colors pop best.

   b. Babysit your little sister; who always has so much fun with you.

   c. Help him program the DVR; you're the only one who gets it.

   d. Put together the new bookcase since you're so good with your hands.

4. **When you were little, your favorite toy was a:**

   a. Plastic microphone. You couldn't wait to sing in sold-out venues.

   b. Doll-sized stethoscope. Fixing your stuffed animals' boo-boos made you feel good.

   c. Microscope. You loved the idea of this whole other world that you couldn't see without a slide.

   d. Kickball. Even then, you liked to be in constant motion.

5. Your favorite cell phone app is called:

a. Artist's Touch. It lets you turn your pics into a work of art.

b. LifeTimer. It helps you keep up with all of your volunteer commitments.

c. Code Sleuth. On the off chance that you don't know what a particular Mac error code means, this app fills you in.

d. Virtual Trainer. You can get your workout on anywhere.

6. If there were a book about your life, it would be called:

a. *Fabulous! A Creative Mind is a Wonderful Thing to Flaunt*

b. *Help! The Story of the Teen Who Loved to Take Care of People*

c. *Ping! A Digital Life is a Life Well-Lived*

d. *Move! How Far I Got by Refusing to Stand Still*

7. Your favorite class is:

a. Drama. You enjoy creating new characters every day.

b. Social studies. You love to learn about the world and how we can make it a better place.

c. Computer lab. You feel like you're actually learning something!

d. Wood shop. You love showing the class how it's *really* done.

8. In your favorite daydream, you are:

a. Moving the world with your art.

b. Winning the Nobel Peace Prize.

c. Proving that life exists on Mars.

d. Completing construction on the country's tallest building.

9. Your favorite color is:

a. Wait, do you have to pick just one?

b. Green. It's just so soothing and mellow.

c. Gunmetal gray, just like all your gear.

d. Black or white. They're straightforward.

10. When your parents want to do something special for you, they:

a. Pass you the credit card and let you go crazy at the art supply store.

b. Make a donation in your name to your fave charity.

c. Give you the cash to update your operating system.

d. Give you free rein to track down the source of that grinding sound under the hood.

Results ➡

If you got mostly As, you're …
The Creator

Forget marching to the beat of your own drum: You're simultaneously playing the drum, wearing a uniform you designed yourself, singing your own lyrics, and taking pictures of your journey. Whether you deal in words, beats, colors, fabrics, or something no one else has ever dabbled in before, your creativity turns everything you touch into a work of art. You find inspiration in everything, and you know how to use it. You can channel your love of all things artsy by considering a business in:

✹ **Clothing design.** Do you make one-of-a-kind threads? Stop being stingy and share your designs with the masses.

✹ **Magazine publishing.** Are you in love with the written word? Put together your own online zine and tell the world about your fondness for indie movies or old school hip-hop.

✹ **Photography.** Have you got an eye for a great picture? Be the official photographer at your friends' b-day parties and get a contract to take shots at school football games.

✹ **Jewelry making.** Is everyone always asking where you get your funky earrings? Create a few more pairs and make a killing.

✹ **Comic book creation.** If you have a knack for writing *and* drawing, creating graphic novels could be your thing.

✹ **Room decorating.** Everybody knows that your room is the most fabulous one in the neighborhood. Bring your knack for decorating to your classmates' abodes.

✹ **Card design.** Do you never see just the right card at the store? Create your own line and sell them online and at school.

✹ **Graphic design.** Put your artistic talent to good use and create flyers and posters for the bands in your school.

✹ **Baking.** Your red velvet cupcakes are too good to keep all to yourself. Bake them for your friends' parties and family functions.

✹ **DJing.** Turn a buck off your hot iPod playlists; no one should enjoy all that musical goodness for free!

If you got mostly Bs, you're …

The Helper

Calling you a "people person" doesn't do you justice. You're a rockstar when it comes to assessing the needs of others and finding ways to assist, and the people in your sphere trust you with their lives. Your spot-on advice is invaluable to those around you. So whether someone is asking how to plan an amazing birthday party or how to get to the other side of an argument with their BFF, they know you can help. It only makes sense to build a company that incorporates aspects of service. You should consider a business in:

✻ **Babysitting.** Why should your parents get to keep all of your yummy meal–making, ankle biter–taming babysitting skills for themselves?

✻ **Hair styling.** Your friends benefit from your haircutting skills. Why wouldn't everyone else?

✻ **Sickie services.** Who makes better chicken noodle soup than you? No one! Deliver homemade soup—and DVDs, books, and cough medicine—to sick people in your neighborhood.

✻ **Tutoring.** Help your classmates ace their finals or teach kids at the elementary school how to navigate the peril that is Miss Schumaker's fifth grade English class.

✻ **House sitting.** Water the plants, take care of pets, and collect the mail when your neighbors are away.

✻ **Closet organizing.** Use your Zen gift to declutter your friends' spaces.

✻ **Wardrobe stylist.** You always look like you just walked off a runway; help your less stylish peers get their game up.

✻ **Party planning.** Your birthday party is consistently the most ridiculous one of the year. Spread the love!

✻ **Errand running.** Do the old and infirm in your area a favor; run their errands and handle their shopping when they can't.

✻ **Pet walking.** From little dogs that look like cats to the occasional iguana, you can walk them or care for them when the owners are too busy.

If you got mostly Cs, you're …

The Techie

You can take a complicated concept like molecular physics and break it down like a hip-hop remix. Your web page has the hottest layout this side of the Mississippi (from scratch, none of that cut-and-paste stuff for you), and you're both a Mac *and* a PC. So it's no surprise that when the adults in your life need help putting music on their iPods or your best friend needs the code to unlock unlimited lives on the latest hot Xbox 360 game, you're the one they call. Use your technical prowess to make your fortune and consider a business in:

✹ **Website creation.** Use videos and blogs to design amazing websites for your friends' bands, zines, and photography galleries.

✹ **Video editing.** Help your friends turn their random video moments into viral masterpieces.

✹ **Computer repair.** Replacing hard drives and adding memory may freak other folks out, but it's all in an afternoon's play for you.

✹ **Video game tournaments.** Organize contests for your die-hard gaming friends and charge an entry fee.

✹ **Software installation.** Upgrade operating systems for people with outdated computers—and computer skills.

✹ **Tech lending library.** You buy the hot games, CDs, and DVDs as soon as they hit the market. Lend them out for a fee and recoup your investment.

✹ **Software tutorials.** Teach kids and grandpas to use word-processing programs and photo-editing software.

✹ **Data backup.** People always say they're going to back up their data, but no one does. Do it for them—and charge a fee.

✹ **System installation.** You've never seen a sound system, car radio, or intercom you couldn't install.

✹ **Equipment rental and sales.** You have more computer mice and RCA cables than you know what to do with. Rent them out (or sell them) and rake in the dough.

SOUTHBOROUGH LIBRARY

Southborough Library
http://www.southboroughlib.org

Checked Out Items 6/27/2016 13:22
CATHERINE DILL

Item Title	Due Date
37374001482823 Explore Boston	7/18/2016 23:59
37374001527064 Pocket Boston	7/18/2016 23:59
37374001482658 Best bike rides Boston : great recreational rides in the metro area	7/18/2016 23:59
37374001239736 Lonely Planet's best in travel	7/18/2016 23:59
37374001533278 Walking Boston : 34 tours through Beantown's cobblestone streets, historic districts, ivory towers and bustling waterfront	7/18/2016 23:59
37374001344270 Start it up : the complete teen business guide to turning your passions into pay	7/18/2016 23:59

Check discs in audiobooks and DVD-sets.

Item Title	Due Date
37374001482823 Explore Boston	7/18/2016 23:59
37374001527064 Pocket Boston	7/18/2016 23:59
37374001482658 Best bike rides Boston : great recreational rides in the metro area	7/18/2016 23:59
37374001239736 Lonely Planet's best in travel	7/18/2016 23:59
37374001533278 Walking Boston : 34 tours through Beantown's cobblestone streets, historic districts, ivory towers and bustling waterfront	7/18/2016 23:59
37374001344270 Start it up : the complete teen business guide to turning your passions into pay	7/18/2016 23:59

Check discs in audiobooks and DVD-sets.

If you got mostly Ds, you're ...
The Handy One

You're no stranger to hard work, and you're happiest when you're using your hands. It started even before wood shop; you were the kid who built a fort in the backyard with stuff scavenged from the garage. If your uncle is moving, he knows you will happily help out. And that entertainment center your mom bought that came in a million pieces? That's all you. You love seeing the concrete results of your labor. Even if you're not amazing at every sport, it just feels good to move your body every day, and you're not afraid to break a sweat or get a little dirty to do it. It'll be easy to start a business that capitalizes on being physical. You should consider a business in:

* **Landscaping:** You love being outdoors, and you've been doing yard work your whole life. Take this show on the road.

* **Moving service:** You do it for your loved ones; why not get paid for schlepping around all those boxes? (Remember: "Thank-you pizza" doesn't count as pay!)

* **Personal training:** Perfect form in the gym comes easy to you. Help your less toned friends get it.

* **Furniture assembly:** Put together countless pieces of Scandinavian-made fake wood using one little Allen wrench. No problem.

* **Personal coaching:** Use your crazy football skills to help young folks make the teams at their schools.

* **Snow removal:** Hat? Check. Gloves? Check. Shovel? Check! You're ready to go clear some walks and dig out some cars for cash.

* **Cleaning service:** You have an affinity for making stuff sparkle. Put it to good use.

* **Car repair:** You know you're good with cars, so make your friends cough up some dough when you get their clunkers running.

* **House painting:** Inside or out, give you a bucket of paint, a few rollers and a ladder, and you can make a space look like new.

* **Skateboard and bicycle repair:** Your skater and BMX friends are always busting their equipment, but you can put it back together better than it was before.

More Than One Type

If you read all the descriptions, you'll notice that there is some overlap among categories. Don't be afraid to cross lines. There are no hard rules; just do what will make you happy. Maybe you got mostly As, but you're actually more of a creative helper. Instead of designing your own clothing line, your best bet might be to help homeless women get back into the workforce by putting together snazzy interview outfits for them using clothing donations and thrift store finds.

Or maybe the quiz says you should be a helper because it's something you're good at, but you'd really rather run video game tournaments. Do it! (Just because you're good with your little siblings doesn't mean you have to devote your career to changing diapers.)

Before we go any further, take a second to cement the idea for your company. Then, write down ▤ your company concept. Be as specific as possible; you'll be referring to it throughout the book.

Resources

YEAbiz.com
This is the website for the Young Entrepreneurs of America. Read start-up stories from other teen CEOs and get inspired ideas for your own company.

Entrepreneur.com/tsu
Check out this site for tons of how-to articles for young entrepreneurs.

TeenEntrepreneurBootcamp .org
Check out this site for info on two-week camps that give you hands-on experience that will help you start your company.

SBA.gov/teens
This section of the Small Business Association site is dedicated to helping teenagers get their businesses off the ground.

The Element: How Finding Your Passion Changes Everything by Ken Robinsonn, with Lou Aronica
Need help pinpointing your passion? This book can help.

How I Started My Business

KODA is an online community that employers and young professionals use to connect. More than 400 employers, including Fortune 500 market leaders, use the site for their entry- to mid-level recruiting needs. The idea began in college when my cofounder, Tony York, and I realized that our generation was lost when it came to finding a job after graduation. The career center was essentially useless, and major job boards are overwhelming when you don't even know what you are looking for. We knew there had to be a better way for college students to connect with employers.

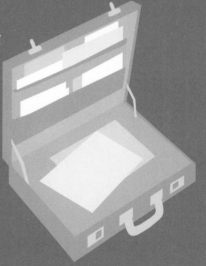

—Jeff Berger, founded employee recruiting portal KODA at age 22

CHAPTER 2

WHO'S GOT YOUR BACK?

Establishing a Support System

Now that you know what business you want to run, you have to figure out who can help you pull it off. Just because it's your business doesn't mean that you have to do *everything* on your own. It's just like your life. Yeah, you're the one who's working hard in the classroom, but your teachers (the good ones) give you tips on how to study for big tests. You might not go out on dates with your friends, but they help you pick out what to wear or decide where to go. Your parents (hopefully) won't be going off to college with you, but they probably have a lot of advice that you'll use when deciding what school to attend. All of these people form your support system, which is essential in the business world. Any great leader will tell you that success is impossible without the help of others.

Find a Mentor

Figuring out all of the things that are needed to start your business can seem like a daunting task, but finding a mentor can make it easier. A mentor is someone who has already started a business and can help you navigate common pitfalls. It could be someone who works in the same industry as you. So if you aspire to create a unique line of hand-painted greeting cards, you might look online for someone who sells her own line of greeting cards. Your mentor could also be someone who works in a completely different area and is just good at business. Most of the skills required to run a company are the same whether you're repairing cars or mowing lawns.

It's surprisingly easy to find a successful businessperson to help you; many entrepreneurs are eager to give advice and guide you through difficult decisions. To find a good mentor, check to see if your school has an entrepreneurship program that can match you with someone. You can also go to Score (Score.org), which is run by retired executives who spend their days doling out useful business advice. This organization also has local centers around the country, so you can even walk in and find someone to help you. Or contact the local branch of Junior Achievement (JA.org); not only will you find a mentor but you can also take free classes and learn everything from how to manage money to the best way to deal with an ethical dilemma.

Once you find a mentor, there are a few things you can do to make the most of your relationship.

✸ **Be proactive.** Your mentor is undoubtedly busy, so it will likely be up to you to keep your relationship going, especially if she has several other people she's mentoring. For that reason, it's unrealistic to always expect her to come to you. Send check-in emails (or make check-in phone calls if that's her thing) to keep her abreast of your progress, and ask for a lunch meeting when you need help. No matter how talented your mentor is, she can't read your mind when you're in distress.

* **Be prepared.** It's important to make the best use of both your time and his. When you set up meetings with your mentor, be sure to have specific topics to discuss and questions you need answered. And then be prepared to take action based upon the feedback you receive.

* **Be open.** You might not always agree with the advice your mentor gives, but it's important to remain open-minded and receptive. For every suggestion she might make that you don't love, there will probably be one that's dead on for you and your business. Remember, she has been where you are and has survived—she had to have learned *something* along the way!

If you're not having any luck finding a suitable mentor—or just want to bounce ideas off of some more people—there are great entrepreneurship groups online where newbies support each other. Meetup (Meetup.com) brings together like-minded people around the world. Just enter your interest (in this case, "entrepreneur") and your ZIP code, and you'll instantly be connected with other business owners in your area. Many of the groups actually meet offline, too. If you decide to attend a meeting, take a parent, older friend, or sibling the first time you go to be sure that it's safe.

> *I met my mentor when I went to hear him speak and told him I wanted to do what he does. He gave me his phone number and said, "Call me this evening, we have things to talk about." I did, and he took me under his wing to show me how to do it.*
>
> *—David Bridgeforth, founded public speaking and lifestyle coaching company Bridgeforth Communications at age 16*

Gather a Board of Advisors

Beyond your mentor, you'll want other people to bounce ideas off of as you move forward. All great companies have a board of advisors. Your advisors are different than your mentor. Typically each advisor contributes some specific expertise to help you run your company (financial savvy, brutal honesty, promotion chops), whereas a mentor serves as a jack-of-all-trades in whose footsteps you can follow. When forming your board of advisors, think about people like your grandmother who *always* tells the truth, your money-savvy aunt or uncle, and your best friend who is on student council and is amazing at convincing your classmates that they *have* to attend every school dance. You don't pay these people; they just help you because they want to see you succeed. Write down who will be in your business inner circle.

To Go Solo or Have a Partner?

One of the first questions that often comes to mind when starting a business is whether or not to work with a partner. The decision depends on two things.

1 Do you have the resources you need to start your business alone? Some partnerships are formed out of financial necessity—you could offer your brother partnership in exchange for giving you

---

Your family and friends are the people who will be the most honest with you. If I ask someone whom I employ, "What do you think about this phrase I came up with?" they might say, "Oh, it's wonderful! It's great!"—even if it's horrible—just because I pay them. But if one of my close friends who helps out reads it, he'll say, "'Chauncey, that's wack." You need that honesty as an entrepreneur.

—Chauncey Holloman, founded greeting card company Harlem Lyrics at age 17

start-up cash. Other partnerships are born because each partner has skills or tools that, when combined, make for a successful business. For example, maybe you want to start a landscaping company. If you have a riding mower and your friend has a pickup truck, it could be a great match. Or perhaps you have notebooks full of comic book storylines and your buddy can draw. You could join forces to create a new series.

2 Do you prefer working alone or with someone else? When you work alone, you are your own boss and you have a lot of independence. But you're also responsible for *everything*, and you need to be self-motivated.

If you're still not sure whether or not to have a partner, weigh the pros and cons on the next page.

The Tip Jar `TIPS`

Prioritize

Running a business takes good time-management skills. There are only so many hours in the day, so you need to prioritize your activities and decide what must get done and what can be delayed or dismissed. To do this, list all the stuff you juggle every week, including school, chores, activities and clubs, socializing, volunteering, sports, and various lessons. Then number them in order of what's most crucial, starting with school. Company or no company, you still need to graduate! Then, put your new business in there. Now you have a guide that'll help you decide when to do what. So if you have a geometry test tomorrow but a client wants you to make a delivery tonight, you'll refer back to your priority list, remember that school comes first, and choose to study before you make your delivery. On the flip side, if soccer practice is the thing that stands in the way but you've ranked your company above soccer, you may need to miss practice.

The Upsides of Going It Alone

☀ **Autonomy.** Hate group projects at school? You probably like to make your own decisions and run with them without having to check in with other people. No partner means total autonomy.

☀ **More money.** If you have a partner, they're going to expect some kind of compensation. Keep the company to yourself, and you don't have to split your profits. Cha-ching!

☀ **Efficiency.** Working with someone else can sometimes feel like a job in and of itself, especially if your partner is slower than you are at getting things done. Working alone could be more efficient.

☀ **Self-satisfaction.** Working alone can be very gratifying. There's something wonderful about knowing that you are able to start a company all by yourself.

The Upsides of Having a Partner

☀ **Collaboration.** The view might be beautiful, but it can be lonely at the top. Working with a friend can make running your own business more fun—and even more creative (two brains are better than one).

☀ **Assistance.** If you really want to design websites, you may not want to spend all of your hours figuring out the intricacies of marketing. Bring a savvy partner on board to get help in areas where you are less of an expert—and have no desire to be.

☀ **Less stress.** Splitting your energy among creating your website, handling customer service issues, and making sure your product is amazing could suck the joy right out of your company. If you can find someone you trust, joining forces can make your life easier.

Partnering Up

If you decide to get a partner, know that lots of great businesses were developed by partnerships. Have you ever eaten Ben & Jerry's ice cream? It's the brainchild of Ben Cohen and Jerry Greenfield, two guys who met in seventh grade gym class and decided to start a company together 14 years later. Sometimes working with a partner can make running a business much easier—and a lot more fun. It's nice to have someone to share the responsibilities with. And when things go really well, you have someone right there with you to celebrate.

Generally, partners put in equal work, get equal pay, and have an equal say in how the company is run. But you can divide the company differently if you want.

(So if you run your data backup company during the school year because your partner belongs to a million clubs, and he runs it in the summer to accommodate your annual trip to your Uncle Albert's farm, you might own 70 percent of the company to his 30 percent and get paid accordingly.) When you do all your official paperwork (more on that in Chapter 4), you'll specify what percentage of the company you each own.

The most important part of working with a partner is picking the right individual. This person is going to be the other face of your project; he can't be a slacker. You'd also be smart to pick someone who has a vision similar to yours. If you're all about starting a housesitting business, but your partner wants to DJ parties, it will be hard to come to an agreement about what your company will look like.

> *My mom is my business partner. Early on, we sat down and separated our jobs. I do the creative stuff, and she handles the logistical stuff. Setting guidelines is really important, especially when it comes to a child-parent run company. It makes it easier because we don't do the same things, so we don't clash as often as people who do everything together.*
>
> *—Chauncey Holloman, founded greeting card company Harlem Lyrics at age 17*

How I Started My Business

Back in 2004, I was trying to figure out what to do to make money. Then my friend said, "We need to start cutting grass." I partnered with him, made some little flyers, and it started going really well. After a couple of weeks, my friend said he wanted to step back from managing the business and just help me out, so I took it over. At first, we just had my father's lawnmower, then we got one from the junkyard and fixed it up. I didn't spend the money I earned on myself—I just kept buying more equipment and reinvesting in the company. So that's pretty much how it kept going.

—Blaine Mickens, founded landscaping company Estate Groomers at age 14

You need to create a unified vision if you're going to make your enterprise a successful one.

Another important consideration is your partner's skill set and interests. It's best if you can find someone who is good at things you aren't and vice versa. For example, if you want to design clothes but hate the idea of personally approaching local boutiques to sell them, it makes sense to bring in a partner who feels at ease promoting your product to people. (The bonus of dividing work like this is that you may also need fewer—if any—staffers if you and your partner can get the whole job done between the two of you.) Excitement also matters. Don't tie yourself financially to someone who thinks being an entrepreneur might be "kinda OK." You need someone who is just as excited about running things as you are.

When choosing whether to work alone or with a partner, there are also financial implications that you'll need to consider. To learn more about those, see page 59 in Chapter 4.

Going It Alone

Want to work alone? It can definitely be done, but you'll have to create a support network to help you cover all the bases because you're going to need help along the way. First, you should make sure your mentor and advisors are in place (see pages 28 and 30). They will be especially helpful if you plan to work alone. Next, you'll need to commit yourself to becoming self-sufficient. Lots of entrepreneurs do everything themselves in the beginning, from customer service to marketing to making deliveries. You'll have to draw on all the skills you posses and use them to get your business off the ground.

> *It's difficult to run a company while I am in school. I have to make sure I balance my class work and my social stuff so I have time to work on my company. I am very lucky to have my dad as a mentor, though; he has been helping me and answering all of my questions.*
>
> *—Alexa Carlin, founded OmniPeace jewelry line Alexa Rose at age 17*

Next Steps

As you set up your company, you may find that you also need a staff, particularly if you have a business like helping college freshmen move into their dorms or painting homes in your neighborhood. When you (and your partner, if you have one) are ready to start hiring people, see Chapter 6 to learn how to do that.

Resources

JA.org

Junior Achievement is an organization dedicated to helping young people start their own businesses. Find a chapter near you and connect with a mentor or sign up for an entrepreneurship course.

Score.org

This nonprofit is run by retired executives who love to give advice to new business owners like you. Get help online or find a local center near you and meet someone face to face.

YoungEntrepreneur.com

This is an online community for new business owners. Visit it for tips and to connect with other entrepreneurially minded teens.

Meetup.com

Go to this site to connect with other entrepreneurs online and even to make plans to meet up and discuss business offline. It's like having your own little support group.

How I Started My Business

On December 14, 2009, best-selling business author Seth Godin released an ebook called What Matters Now. It featured big ideas from some of the most interesting and accomplished people in the world. My friend and I downloaded it and swallowed the book whole, reveling in its insight and inspiration. Then we had the great idea to create another ebook filled with contributions from the younger generation. So I asked Seth, and he said, "Great idea! Go do it!" So I emailed some friends, and together we created What's Next? It is a guide for young change-makers, entrepreneurs, and activists to help them share their big ideas. The ebook is free, and a paid print edition benefits charity. We also created a companion website that offers consulting services to young professionals. Young people have big ideas and big dreams, and they're doing creative things to carry out their vision for the world, but their voices aren't always heard. We want to give them a platform to speak out and inspire other teens, parents, and educators.

—Crystal Yan, founded book project What's Next: 25 Big Ideas from Gen-Yers Under 25 at age 17

CHAPTER 3

GETTING SERIOUS

Creating a Business Plan

You want to have a business? You need a business plan. Don't let the official-sounding name freak you out: It's really just writing down what your business is, what you want it to become, and how you plan to get there. You'll start it in this chapter and continue working on it as you go through the book. If you take it step by step, it's a breeze.

A business plan details what your goals are, where your money is, and where your money isn't. It tells you what to charge for services and how much to pay people, and it comes in handy if you're going to ask your parents (or anyone) for a loan. When they read it, they should be able to tell exactly what you're planning to do with their money and how long it will take to pay them back. It's the step that many entrepreneurs skip when they're starting out, but stepping up to the plate now will help you hit a home run later.

Plan It and Plan to Change It

While it's important to create a business plan before you buy supplies and hire employees, it's also important to understand that your business plan might change after your company gets going. Sometimes you'll find that the choice you made in the beginning no longer makes sense. For example, maybe you figured you could run the business yourself, but people are now clamoring for your room design service, and you just don't have enough time to take on all those clients yourself. Because it's *your* business, *you* can make the decision to deviate from your original plan and hire a helper to do initial evaluations for you so you have more time to do the actual space design. You may also encounter situations that you didn't anticipate in the planning stage and that your business plan doesn't account for. Maybe your business plan only talks about room design, but someone has asked you to design the interior of an entire house. You'll need to evaluate the situation and add the new policy to your business plan. Bottom line: Your business plan should grow and change right along with your company.

> *I never planned when I first started. I just went with what I felt was right. But now I plan a lot. It gives you foresight into how you want the business to turn out and a better chance of succeeding. Without creating a business plan, you don't really consider all the details and the possibilities. It's like when I put together a website without thoroughly planning: It never gets to where I want it to be.*
>
> —Donny Ouyang, founded website development and marketing company Kinksaro Tech Limited at age 13

Step by Step

So, what goes into your business plan? Well, a ton of stuff. Your business plan will include information on your company's mission, who will help you execute your vision, how you will operate from day to day, where you will get your funding, how much you will charge for your products or services, who will buy what you're selling, how you will let people know about your company, and how you will use your company to make the world a better place. It may sound like a lot, but the great thing is that everything you need to know for your business plan can be generated from reading this book and using the notes you are making in your notebook. Ready to get started? Have a look at the sample business plan on pages 42–49.

The Tip Jar TIPS

Hit "Save As"

As your business grows and changes, it's only normal that you will make tweaks to your business plan. But don't get rid of the old versions; you never know when you might need to refer back to them. Instead, make a copy and save your changes in the new version. Change the file name by adding today's date to the end or by calling it Version 2. That way, if you suddenly realize that one of your old ideas that didn't work last year might work *now*, you won't drive yourself nuts (and waste all kinds of time) trying to conjure up all the details.

Sample Business Plan

Here's a sample business plan. You can photocopy it or type it up if you don't want to write in the book or if you want to be able to make changes to it later on. The chapters listed on the right side of each line indicate where in the book these topics are discussed. Have a look and see what we've already covered and fill that in. Then continue reading the book to get the information for the rest.

Business Description

My business is called _____ (Chapter 4).

The company's website is _____ (Chapter 4).

The company's mission is to _____

_____ (Chapter 1).

The services my company will provide are _____

_____

_____

_____ (Chapter 1).

My business is important to the market right now because

_____

_____

_____

_____ (Chapter 7).

Management Team

My board of advisors will include:

_____, _____, _____,

_____, _____, _____ (Chapter 2).

I, _____, will run this company (along with my

partner_____) (Chapter 2).

My title is/our titles are_____ (Chapter 6).

I/we will earn $ _____ (Chapters 5 and 6).

My staff/contract workers will include:

Name: _____ (Chapter 6)

Role: _____ (Chapter 6)

Pay/salary: $_____ (Chapters 5 and 6)

Name: _____ (Chapter 6)

Role: _____ (Chapter 6)

Pay/salary: $_____ (Chapters 5 and 6)

Name: _____ (Chapter 6)

Role: _____ (Chapter 6)

Pay/salary: $_____ (Chapters 5 and 6)

Continued ➡

Business Operations

My company's legal structure will be_____ (Chapter 4).

My business address is _____

and it is registered in the city and state of _____ (Chapter 4).

Financials

My business' start-up costs will total _____(Chapter 4).

The details are below:

Legal fees _____ (Chapter 4).

Registrations and licenses _____ (Chapter 4).

Equipment _____ (Chapter 5).

Certifications_____ (Chapter 5).

Other _____ (Chapter 5).

My business' operating costs will total _____ (Chapter 5).

The details are below:

Space rental_____ (Chapter 5).

Website _____ (Chapter 4).

Ongoing training _____ (Chapter 5).

Supplies_____ (Chapter 5).

Transportation _____ (Chapter 5).

Advertising_____ (Chapter 5).

Employee compensation _____(Chapters 5 and 6).

Insurance _____ (Chapter 5).

Other _____ (Chapter 5).

My funding will come from the following sources:

Savings $ _____ (Chapter 5).

Partner $_____ from _____ (Chapter 5).

Gifts $_____ from _____ (Chapter 5).

Grants $_____ from _____ (Chapter 5).

Loans $_____ from _____ (Chapter 5).

Investors $_____ from _____ (Chapter 5).

Other   _____ (Chapter 5).

My company will charge the following prices:

Service/product 1 $_____ for _____ (Chapter 5).

Service/product 2 $_____ for _____ (Chapter 5).

Service/product 3 $_____ for _____ (Chapter 5).

Service/product 4 $_____ for _____ (Chapter 5).

Service/product 5 $_____ for _____ (Chapter 5).

Service/product 6 $_____ for _____ (Chapter 5).

Continued ➡

Budget Worksheet

Here is a projected monthly budget of our income, expenses, and profit for the first year (Chapter 5).

	JAN	FEB	MAR	APR	MAY	JUN	JUL	AUG	SEP	OCT	NOV	DEC	Total
1. Number of jobs done/ items sold													
2. Average price per job/item													
3. Total income (row 1 x row 2)													
4. Average expense for each job/item													
5. Total expense per job/ item (row 1 x row 5)													
6. Other monthly operating costs													
7. Total expense (row 6 + row 7)													
8. Profit/loss before taxes (row 3 – row 8)													

(Note: The chart above will detail your finances for your first year—or how ever many months you choose to show. You will estimate these numbers in Chapter 5. Let's say you're filling out the column for January. In row 1, you'll write how many jobs you think you'll complete or products you think you'll sell. In row 2, you'll write how much you will charge for each. To complete row 3, you'll multiply the numbers from rows 1 and 2. Fill out the rest of the rows using the directions down the left side of the chart.)

Market Analysis

My local competitors are: _____ (Chapters 5 and 7)

My product/service is different in the following ways:

1. _____ (Chapters 5 and 6).

2. _____ (Chapters 5 and 6).

3. _____ (Chapters 5 and 6).

There are several audiences who are primed to purchase my service or product. They are:

1. _____because _____

_____(Chapter 7).

2. _____because _____

_____(Chapter 7).

3. _____because _____

_____(Chapter 7).

Marketing Plan

My customers can be found in the following real and virtual locations:

1. _____(Chapter 7).

2. _____(Chapter 7).

3. _____(Chapter 7).

4. _____(Chapter 7).

Continued ➡

My marketing strategy will include the following low- and high-tech methods of reaching my potential customers:

1. _____
   _____ (Chapter 7).

2. _____
   _____ (Chapter 7).

3. _____
   _____ (Chapter 7).

4. _____
   _____ (Chapter 7).

Giving Back Plan

My company is committed to giving back to the community that supports us. We will give $_____ each year/month (circle one) **to the following causes:**

1. _____ (Chapter 9).

2. _____ (Chapter 9).

3. _____ (Chapter 9).

We will participate in the following activities that will help our community:

1. _____ (Chapter 9).

2. _____ (Chapter 9).

3. _____ (Chapter 9).

We will take the following steps to mentor other young entrepreneurs:

1. _____

   _____ (Chapter 9).

2. _____

   _____ (Chapter 9).

3. _____

   _____ (Chapter 9).

4. _____

   _____ (Chapter 9).

We will adopt the following environmentally friendly business practices:

1. _____

   _____ (Chapter 9).

2. _____

   _____ (Chapter 9).

3. _____

   _____ (Chapter 9).

4. _____

   _____ (Chapter 9).

How I Started My Business

I love to dance, and I've been taking classes—jazz, tap, hip-hop, lyrical, ballet, salsa, merengue, contemporary modern—since I was two. I started my company to share my dance talents with younger and underprivileged children. On September 6, 2008, I woke up at 1:02 in the morning with the idea for my dance school. I ran and woke up my mom. She told me to go back to bed, but I insisted that I needed a pink bus. And she said, "Why do you need a bus?" I told her that I could teach kids to dance inside this bus. I wanted to fight the obesity epidemic in America, and dancing is a fun way to exercise. And she said, "OK, I'll get you this crazy bus if you just let me go back to sleep."

I got the bus for Christmas. We painted it pink, ripped out the seats, installed a dance floor, mirrors, and a barre, and started teaching classes the next month. We contract with schools, then park the bus there for an hour a week after school and teach whatever types of dance they choose. I have a director and three instructors, and I teach dance classes when I can, like during summers and when I don't have any homework. The money from this will help pay for Harvard Medical School so I can be an obstetrician.

—Amiya Alexander, founded Amiya's Mobile Dance Academy at age 10

I wrote my first business plan in a high school course, and it became my road map. I think it's good to figure out exactly what you're out to accomplish and to go through the steps necessary to make it happen.

—Chelsea Rustrum, founded web aggregation company Free Mania at age 14

Resources

Score.org
This site, which was mentioned in Chapter 2 as a great place to find a mentor, also offers free planning tools for small business owners, like super-comprehensive templates for business plans and financial projections.

Entrepreneur.com/businessplan
This site walks you through the process of creating a detailed business plan.

SBA.gov/smallbusinessplanner/plan/writeabusinessplan
This section of the Small Business Administration site has tons of resources to help you develop all aspects of your business plan.

CHAPTER 4

THE TECHNICAL STUFF

Making Your Business Official

So you're ready to start your company. You've come up with the concept, started your business plan, and put into place a team of advisors and even a mentor or two who has been there, done everything. Now it's time for the cool part: making it official. That means choosing the perfect name for your business, getting it registered, and doing all of the paperwork needed to make it legit. It can be a lot of work, but it's better to do this right now than to put it off until later when you're so busy running your business that it might *never* get done.

Step by Step

There are a lot of technical things involved in making your business official, but it all comes down to these six easy steps.

Step 1: Come Up With a Name

First thing's first: You need to pick a company name. Before people know anything about your company, they will know its name, so now is not the time to be lazy. It might be tempting to stick your own name in there (Larry's Landscaping, Pauline's Paintings, and what have you), and that's fine, but just be sure that the name you choose does more than just shamelessly self-promote. That means that putting "Larry Rules" on the side of the old pickup truck you'll use to transport your lawnmowers might not be the best idea because the only message it conveys is that you're awesome, not that you're awesome at cutting grass. Coming up with a name is tricky.

To start, brainstorm a company name. This is where you come up with a few options. Here are some tips.

✹ **Make it relevant.** In short, it needs to make sense. If you want to be a personal shopper and wardrobe stylist for girls at your school, your business shouldn't be called Peggy's Cupcakes. Yeah, maybe you love cupcakes or your favorite dress is pink like yummy frosting, but that doesn't have anything to do with what your business does. Styling by Peggy is a much more relevant name.

✹ **Make it memorable.** You don't want it to blend in. If there are three other girls at your school who babysit, you don't want to get lost in the crowd. While one girl may call her business The Babysitter, you can blow her out of the water with a name like Babies Love Candy (particularly if your name is Candy). Get creative with it.

✹ **Make it pass the "scrunch test."** Your name needs to make immediate sense. If people squint their eyes, purse their lips, tilt their heads, or scrunch their faces when they hear your company name, you're in trouble. Ditto if they have a difficult time saying it. Pick something that is clear, simple to pronounce and spell, and rolls easily off the tongue.

Once you have a few ideas, write them down. ▣ Have a few choices because you may need some backups. Then, test drive them to make sure they're really as great as you think. Here's where your advisors and employees come in. Whether you get them all together to discuss the pros and cons of the names or survey them each individually, don't skip this step. How else will you realize that the name that sounds perfect to your ear is hard to pronounce or sounds like a dirty word when you say it quickly? You can even ask potential customers to see what they think before you move forward.

My business has gone through so many names. We started by using the title of my book, You're Grounded! *But we soon found that it was confusing and sounded too negative. Then we used On Teens Today, but that made it sound like the company was only for teens. (It was also very similar to the name of a porn website. We changed that right away!) We picked Radical Parenting two years ago and have stuck with it. I love this name because it shows that we have a completely different approach in the way that we offer parenting advice to families and youth.*

—Vanessa Van Patten, founded teen-run parenting advice company Radical Parenting at age 16

While you are doing all of this, you should see if the names you like are trademarked by someone else or if somebody already has a website connected with them. If your fave name is trademarked already, you could get into a legal mess if you use the same name. And if someone has a website with your company's name on it, you'll lose customers every time people go there instead.

To see if anyone else has already trademarked your business name, get online and enter "Trademark Electronic Search System (TESS) database" in the search box on any browser. You'll get a link to the page of the United States Patent and Trademark Office website, which allows you to type in your company name and check to see if it is taken or free. You may need to change your company name until you find one that no one else has trademarked; keep typing in your backup names until you have a keeper. It's free to run this search.

At the same time, you should be checking to see if the name you like is also available as a domain name for your website. To do this, go to CheckDomain.com and keep typing in names until you find something that is available. You should match your business name as closely as possible. So if you settled on Babies Love Candy, buy babieslovecandy.com if you can. And remember, you can add a location or other identifier to your website name to increase the chances of it being available. For instance, if your New York–based moving company is called Move Easy but there is already a moveeasy.com, you can try moveeasyNY.com.

Coming up with a name that works and is available for trademark and for a new website can take some time. Keep repeating the above process until you find a name that's both perfect and available. When you are ready to move forward and trademark your name, and buy the domain name for the site, go to Steps 2 and 3.

Step 2: Trademark Your Name

On the United States Patent and Trademark Office website, which you visited to see if your name was already trademarked, you'll find the "Initial Application Form" link on the Trademark

My company is called Estate Groomers now, but the original name was Lawn Groomers. When I first came up with it back in 2004, I did a search and nobody had it. I thought everything was good, so I started using it, but I didn't trademark it. I figured I'd do it later. I was just happy to be making money, and all the rest of the stuff seemed irrelevant. But when I went to trademark it in 2007, I found out that somebody had just taken it, and I had to go back to the drawing board. It can save you a lot of headaches if you do it now rather than later because you never know. I was fortunate enough not to lose any business, but it's very possible to not only lose business but to lose business to your competitor—especially if they use the same name you did. As a matter of fact, you should do all the paperwork—business license, tax ID number—right away. Having your paperwork in order will make people take you more seriously. That's one of the fundamental things that can differentiate you as a young entrepreneur; it provides another layer of trust that makes people more willing to work with you.

—Blaine Mickens, founded landscaping company Estate Groomers at age 14

Electronic Application System (TEAS) page. You can also trademark a logo here. If possible, you should trademark your logo and your name at the same time because it's cheaper than doing them separately. The online form to trademark stuff is a little dense, so you might want to ask your parents or mentor for help. There is a fee, too, so now is the time to dip into your savings (or your parents' pockets) for your initial start-up money. It generally takes about three months to hear if the government has approved your registration. Meanwhile, you can go ahead and start using your fabulous company name. If the feds don't approve it, you'll have to pick another name and apply again—but that probably won't happen if your name is available.

Step 3: Snag a Website

Now is the time to secure your website domain name for your company—even if you aren't yet ready to build your site. Buy the domain name from a registration site like GoDaddy.com or Google.com/a/cpanel/domain, and then pick a hosting site, which is where your website will live, and pay the annual fee. Once you've done all of this, write down your company's domain name and any passwords you'll need to access its registration and hosting sites.

Step 4: Legally Structure Your Business

Your company's legal structure determines who will technically own your company, and it's important to file the papers that make the ownership legit. Will you be the sole owner? You and your partner? A board of people, like the huge businesses that you see on the news?

Which legal structure you'll use depends on your financial needs, how much control you want to have, and your company goals. Though most small business start as sole proprietorships (see definition below) or partnerships, it's very common to restructure as your company grows, so you should know about all the options. And check out Business.gov, a great, free, government-run website that can help you pick the best structure for you. You can also ask your parents to consult a lawyer to help make this important decision or check out LegalZoom.com, a site that guides you and files the appropriate paperwork for you for a fee.

Here is a quick overview of the most common business legal structures. Once you decide which legal structure is best for your company, write it in your notebook.

LEGAL STRUCTURE	DESCRIPTION	THE PROS	THE CONS
Sole proprietorship/partnership	You (and your partner, if you have one) are responsible for everything involved with running the company, from putting together the start-up money to making all the business operations decisions.	This structure requires the least amount of government paperwork to complete both at start-up and tax time. It is the least expensive because you rarely need a lawyer and have fewer paperwork filing fees. You make your own decisions.	It doesn't separate company money from personal money, so you're personally responsible for any financial issues and debt (money owed).
Limited liability company (LLC)	An LLC is a cross between a sole proprietorship and a corporation. You are not personally liable, but you also don't have to do all the paperwork involved in running a corporation.	You are not personally responsible for the company's debt. It requires less paperwork and legwork than starting a corporation (no board members or annual meetings needed).	More expensive than a sole proprietorship to start, an LLC requires you to pay fees to your state to set it up. It requires additional start-up and tax forms that a sole proprietorship doesn't.
Corporation	Your company is owned by a board of stockholders—people who buy a small stake in your company and therefore get to weigh in on big decisions. Meanwhile you run the day-to-day operations. The board then pays you a salary.	Your personal money is separate from the company's money, so you are not liable for financial issues. You can sell stock to raise funds.	A corporation takes a lot of work and legal paperwork to start. You have to find a board of people who are willing to buy a stake in your company. You can't make big decisions (such as where you operate) on your own. Though the board pays to run the company later, this is the most expensive option up front because of the fees you have to pay to set up a corporation, the additional annual tax paperwork, and costs involved with holding board meetings.

How I Started My Business

I love to talk, and I want to show people what's possible in life. I love being able to say something that can make a difference. When I was 15, I went to see the famous motivational speaker Les Brown. He was doing what I wanted to do for a living, and I waited in line for almost six hours after his speech to have a real conversation with him. Finally, there was no one there but his assistant and security, and I walked up to him and said, "Hi, Mr. Brown. I'm David Bridgeforth. I'm 15 years old, and I want to be a speaker like you." He said, "I know who you are. You've been following me around all day! What do you want?" I said, "I want to talk to you." He gave me his cell phone number, I called, and the next thing I knew he had arranged for my mom and me to attend his speakers' training for free! He made me speak for 20 minutes on my first day. I got two standing ovations, and a woman offered me the largest amount of money I had ever made for a speech. My grandparents helped me start my own business, and I went on tour with him. Six years later, here I am. I give two or three speeches a month, hold workshops, teach clients how to communicate effectively, and sell products like motivational CDs and DVDs.

—David Bridgeforth, founded public speaking and lifestyle coaching company Bridgeforth Communications at age 16

Step 5: License and Registration

No matter which legal structure you pick, you'll need to register your company's name and apply for a business license, which basically gives you permission to sell stuff to people. To register your business name with your state, go to Business.gov. It will direct you to the website for your particular state and will walk you through all the forms you need to file. Just click on "Register a Business," then click on "Business Licenses and Permits," enter your ZIP code, and select your business category. Select "General Licensing" if none of the other categories apply to your business. The site will pull up instructions, links, and forms for you. Certain types of companies (such as child care) require specialized permits, too, so be sure to cover all your bases.

Note that registering your company is different than trademarking your business name with the federal government, and the process is much easier. You'll need to complete this step before you open a bank account for your company. And if you go with a corporation or LLC, you'll need to file incorporation papers with (and pay incorporation fees

to) your state as well, which sets up your business as its own legal and financial entity separate from you.

Step 6: Set Up Your Business for Tax Purposes

Taxes are a percentage of your income that you pay to the government to help fund things like public schools, parks, roads, and sanitation, to name a few. Yes, you still have to pay them even if you're under 18. To make sure that the government knows about your business and can properly tax you, you need to file some paperwork with both the federal (national) government and the state (and sometimes even your city) when you start your business. Here is a quick overview of what you have to do.

✸ **Apply for a federal employer identification number (EIN).** Unless you are running a sole proprietorship and won't be paying anyone other than yourself, you need to apply for a federal employer identification number (EIN) with the Internal Revenue Service (better known as the IRS, the national agency that collects taxes from individual people and companies every year in the

United States). It's kind of like a social security number for a business; you'll use it to identify your company at tax time to open bank accounts, and to apply for any loans. (Note: If you're the only person on the payroll, you will just file taxes as an individual and pay self-employment tax on your business income—no EIN necessary.) To apply, search for "EIN" on IRS.gov and follow the instructions.

 Register with your state's revenue service. There you will find forms that set you up to charge sales tax (you'll need that if you sell actual products, such as comic books or greeting cards) and to pay taxes on money you pay to employees. Find a link to your state's revenue service at Business.gov under the "State & Local" link.

All of this work sets up your business to be legitimate with the government, but

The Tip Jar — TIPS

File it!

The biggest time suck with taxes comes from not having all of your papers in order. The easiest way to avoid having to search for a receipt in a pile of smelly clothes is to start a filing system before you even think you need one. You should have one for hard copies of receipts and other papers (it can be as simple as a cardboard file box under your bed) and one on your computer for soft copies. Make folders (both paper ones and on your computer) for all the important stuff, like your trademark paperwork, business licenses, bank info, receipts, vendor contact info, etc. When it's time to do your company's taxes, you'll have everything you need, neat and organized. As an added bonus, make files for each client, too, with contact info, past orders, and preferences. That way, when you want to call a client to check in about how his new website (that you built) is working, you won't have to go crazy looking for his number or the details of the project.

it's not the end of the paperwork! Every year, you'll need to report your income to the government and pay taxes on what you earned. Just as your parents probably see an accountant every year at tax time, you may want to hire someone to handle your company's taxes, too, especially if you're not an accounting whiz. Your parents' accountant may agree to do your taxes as well—for a discount. If your

Resources

USPTO.gov/smallbusiness/trademarks
The United States Patent and Trademark Office is the place to go to trademark your company name.

Business.gov
This is a great resource for information on legal business structures, tax issues, and state registrations. It also provides links to every form you need to file to start a business in your state.

LegalZoom.com
This site is like an online lawyer. It will file all your forms for you for a fee. This is a good alternative to hiring some guy in a suit if you're on a budget but would rather not do it yourself.

IRS.gov
At this online home of the Internal Revenue Service (IRS), you can file federal tax forms.

BankRate.com
Search for "state taxes" to see an interactive map that lists state income and sales tax rates.

CheckDomain.com
This free site lets you determine if someone else is already using your domain name idea.

GoDaddy.com
Buy a domain name from this site.

Google.com/a/cpanel/domain
Buy inexpensive domain names here that can easily be integrated with free Google apps, like Gmail and Google.

CHAPTER 5

MONEY MATTERS

How to Amass and Protect Your Fortune

You may have heard that old saying, "You have to spend money to make money." It's still hanging around because it's true. While you can totally start your business on a relatively small budget, you still need a budget. That means figuring out how much dough it will take you to get things off the ground so that you can eventually start to make a profit, calculate where that money will come from, and then figure out what to do with the profit once you start making it. (For instance, it might be tempting to go on a shopping spree, but that will definitely hurt your business!) The bottom line is that to stay in business and to keep doing the thing you love, you need to learn how to earn, manage, and spend your money wisely.

Estimating Your Capital Needs

To run a new business, you need capital, which basically means the money it takes to start and maintain your business. It will likely take you a while to make enough money for your business to be self-sustaining or profitable, so it's important to collect enough capital in the beginning to keep you going for a while. Start by figuring out your capital needs for the first three months of your business. You can always use those numbers to estimate how much you need for a longer period of time. There are two basic costs you'll need to estimate: Start-up costs and operating costs, also known as expenses.

1 **Start-up costs.** These are the things you need to pay for to get your business off the ground. They may be material things (like a new lawnmower and gas for your dad's truck if you're cutting lawns), education in skills that will make you better at what you do (like infant CPR certification for your babysitting business), or the $50 you paid your artsy friend to design your logo. They also include any legal costs you may have incurred in Chapter 4, like fees for trademarking your business name, buying a website domain, hiring a lawyer, or using a paid website to file legal forms. Write down all of your start-up costs.

2 **Operating costs.** These are the things you have to pay for on a regular basis to run your business after you've started it. It's good to have at least enough money on hand to cover them for the first three months. There are two types of operating costs: direct and indirect.

✹ **Direct operating costs** are those related directly to how many products you sell or how many projects you take on. So if you sell homemade cupcakes, you'll need at least enough money to cover ingredients, paper baking cups, decorations, and boxes for each order. These costs also include employee pay, delivery costs (i.e., gas money if you're driving), and anything else associated with getting your product out. Do some research online to see how low you can get these costs. Perhaps you can get a used silk screen printing machine on Craigslist or buy jewelry-making supplies in bulk at the local craft store. Be creative. Then, when you have some figures, estimate your direct operating costs for three months, including the amount you think you'll need to pay employees (more on that on page 89 in Chapter 6). 📓

❋ **Indirect operating costs** (also called overhead) are for things not directly related to selling your product, like location costs and insurance costs.

- Location costs are the money you spend on your workplace. Maybe your parents have no problem with your camping out in their kitchen to make your cupcake confections, so you'll have no location costs. But if your home kitchen is too tiny to turn out huge batches, can you pay your aunt a small fee to use her state-of-the-art double ovens? If you need a space other than your room, think about asking for an empty classroom at school to tutor students, your dad's basement for your clothing design business, or your apartment building's community room for your video game tournaments.

After you decide on your location, write down what it'll cost to use it for three months. 📓

- Insurance costs pay for insurance and warranties that protect you and your company in case the worst happens. Say you design concert posters, and your computer dies the week before you have two projects due. If you have insurance on your computer, you can replace it and get the job done. If not, you're probably going to lose some clients. Here's what you need to know about insurance and its close friend, warranties.

a) Homeowners insurance. **Ask your parents to put your business items on their homeowners' or renters' policy. This will protect you in case something happens in your house. If someone breaks in and steals your hair styling supplies or a fire wipes out your DVD lending library, insurance will pay to replace it all.**

b) Warranties. **Check for extended warranties for items you use for your business. If you bought a computer this summer to start designing, spring for the extended warranty. You'll be glad you did if it crashes.**

c) Car Insurance. If you use your car for your business—say to deliver homemade soup, pick up little kids from school, or run errands—you should spring for full coverage so you don't lose your ability to make cash in the event of an accident.

d) Liability Insurance. If you run a business that involves dealing with people or their personal stuff (think: moving, babysitting, or house cleaning), you should consider this coverage, which protects your business if property is damaged or if there's an accident.

Talk to your parents about which of these you already have and which ones you should get. You can usually buy insurance pretty inexpensively if your family already purchases policies from an agent. Work out what your insurance and warranty costs will be for the first three months. 📓

Add up your start-up costs and your operating costs, both direct and indirect. 📓 You have officially figured out the amount of dough you'll need to keep your business running for the first three months.

> *Raising money can be very hard and time consuming. After a while you might feel like the money you're earning isn't making a big impact, but you should always keep your goal in mind. It costs a lot of money to start a business, but if you really want it, just keep working hard because, in the end, the time, effort, and money you put in will be well worth it.*
>
> *—Alexa Carlin, founded OmniPeace jewelry line Alexa Rose at age 17*

How I Started My Business

I was always a bargain hunter by nature. When I was six years old, I'd tell my mom what was cheaper by the ounce at the grocery store. When the internet first graced our household in 1997—I was 14—the first thing I typed into the search engine was "free stuff." There was only a handful of freebie sites at the time, so it just seemed natural to start Free Mania, which is an online portal for free stuff, product samples, and printable coupons.

—Chelsea Rustrum, founded web aggregation company Free Mania at age 14

Raising Capital

Now you know how much money you need to get your business off the ground. But maybe you don't have it. This is pretty common for new companies. Once your business gets going, it should pay for itself and then some. Until then, you need cash to get—and keep—the ball rolling. Most entrepreneurs get funds from their family and friends, but there are several ways you can raise capital. Here is the deal on the most popular ones.

THE SOURCE	TAPPING INTO IT	THE PROS	THE CONS
Savings	Got a bundle socked away from last year's birthday cards? Now could be a great time to dig it out of that shoebox in the back of your closet.	You don't have to ask anyone for help to finance your business. You can get started immediately.	Bye-bye, new car.
Paychecks	Got a mall job you're dying to quit? Hang on for a few months and stockpile your cash until you have enough to cover your first three months of expenses. Or do a couple of unofficial gigs related to your business (babysitting, web design, etc.) and use the money to finance your official launch.	You don't have to ask anyone for help to finance your business. You can get some work experience under your belt before launch.	You may have to stay at that sucky after-school job just a little while longer if your personal gigs aren't enough.
Partner	If you have some of the money you need and your hardworking, entrepreneurially minded friend has the rest, you could team up to run the business together.	You don't have to finance the business alone.	You have to share the profits. You can't make all the decisions on your own.

THE SOURCE	TAPPING INTO IT	THE PROS	THE CONS
Gifts and grants	Gifts and grants are basically free money to start your business. Ask your old rich uncle or apply to state and federal programs or entrepreneurship competitions to win funds. (See the Resources section at the end of this chapter for more info.)	Free money! You don't have to pay it back.	You actually have to *ask* for gifts, which is sometimes awkward. You need to create your business plan before you ask, even if you're just begging your mom. For grants, you have to complete applications or write proposals to win funds. There is fierce competition for grant money.
Loans	Friends, family, business people, banks, or even complete strangers (see microfinancing info in Resources) who believe in your vision give you money to get things started, and you pay it back at a specified time.	You don't have to come up with funds on your own.	You have to prove to lenders that you are responsible enough to pay back the loans. That includes having a completed business plan to share. You have to pay the money back. If the loan comes with interest you could end up paying back more than you borrowed.
Investors	People who believe that your company will flourish invest in exchange for a percentage of your business. They generally get a say in your business operations because the better you do, the more money they stand to make.	You don't have to come up with funds on your own.	Unless you stipulate otherwise, investors usually have a say in how you run the business. If you sell your company, you'll have to share the profits with your investors.

How will you get the money you need to start your business and run it until you turn a profit? Brainstorm some ideas, including who might be willing to lend you cash and how much.

How to Ask?

Now comes the hard part: If you've decided to go with a loan or an investor who buys a stake in your business, you have to ask someone to give up their hard-earned money to finance your dream. The most important thing is to be prepared. You've already figured out exactly how much you need to get started and to run your business. After you've established how much you expect to pull in (see pages 74–76), you'll be able to determine how long it will take to make enough money to pay back those kind souls.

For example, if you borrow $600 to start your cupcake business, how many batches of $15-per-dozen cupcakes do you need to sell to pay back the loan? And how long do you think it will take to sell them? If your operating costs are $5, one batch gives you a profit of $10 each. $600 / $10 = 60 batches. If you anticipate selling an average of five dozen cupcakes a week, it will take you 12 weeks to make $600 in profits (60/5 = 12 weeks) plus one week to make enough money to finance your first loan-free orders. So it will take you 13 weeks to pay back the investment and to have some money (about $50) to keep you going on your own. But you might want to extend the time to make sure you aren't cutting it too close; you can tell your investor that you can repay the investment in 20 weeks to give yourself a nice cushion.

Once you calculate the payback time and you've completed your business plan that shows how amazing your company is, you can pop the question. Here is a sample script to get you started, whether you're begging your dad or your wealthy mentor. Note that this script works to ask for gifts, too, with a few modifications—just don't offer to pay it back! And if you're going to a bank, take your business plan and your most confident smile; a banker will guide you through the process.

You: Hi, how are you?

Parent/mentor: Good, I'm having a great day! *[If your potential lender is in a bad mood, abort mission and try again some other time.]*

You: Terrific. So you know how I have that idea for a new business?

Parent/mentor: Yeah, it sounds like a smart way for you to make money.

You: I'm glad you think so. I've worked really hard to put together my business plan, and I'd like to ask you to take a look. *[Hand over your business plan.]* The financials show that I'm going to turn a profit pretty quickly. If you agree, would you be willing to loan me the funds to get me started? If all goes according to plan, I'll be able to pay you back the full investment in six months.

Parent/mentor: I can't believe you've done all this work! I'd be happy to take a look and let you know.

Fingers crossed! When you get a yes (because who could possibly resist you?), pull together an agreement that states your names, the date, your state, how much you'll get, and when and how you'll pay it back. Here is a super simple template:

LOAN AGREEMENT

On _____ (date), in the state of _____ (your state), I, _____(your name), will borrow $_____ from _____(lender).

I, _____(your name), agree to repay this loan to _____(lender) by _____. I will make payments of $_____ every _____ (how often you will make payments).

The borrower and lender both agree to the terms as described above.

_____   _____
Borrower's signature   Lender's signature

> *I would suggest starting small, then leveraging your work to get the financing you need. You have to create a track record that will show that what you're doing is successful, then present it to a bank or to your friends and family. That's how you earn the trust of people. No one is going to just say, "OK you have a good idea," and invest in you. You have to prove yourself before you even think about asking for money.*
>
> —Blaine Mickens, founded landscaping company
> Estate Groomers at age 14

Earning Money

OK, now it's time to figure out how much you're going to charge. Setting prices is something that many entrepreneurs have a difficult time doing, but you've already laid the groundwork. There are several things—both tangible and intangible—that you need to consider when determining how much to charge for your service or product.

✹ **Financial goals.** First, you need to figure out how much you want to bank at the end of each week. This is really about setting a financial goal. Do you just want to earn enough to be able to keep making your art? Or do you want to be able to not ask your dad for handouts every week? Are you saving up for college? Itching to be a multimillionaire by the time you're 30? People's goals vary a lot, but if you don't set any goals for your business, you won't make any money. Take some time right now to consider what you want to get from this venture financially. Your goals can—and probably will—change as you go along, and that's fine. It's just good to have a starting point in mind. Spend time thinking about your financial goals and write down your top three.

You should factor them in when you consider the rest of the points below.

❋ **Expenses.** This part is easy because you've already worked on it. One thing you know is that your prices have to be high enough to cover your expenses. So if it costs $5 to produce a dozen cupcakes (including the ingredients, space rental, delivery, and any taxes on those expenses), you must charge more than $5 a batch to turn a profit. If you are still paying off some of your start-up costs, add that into the equation as well. Add up all your expenses.

Then figure out how much each individual job or hour of work will cost you.

❋ **Time value.** Now you need to figure out what your time is worth. If it takes an hour on average to make and deliver a dozen cupcakes, how much do you want to earn in an hour? You could start by looking at the minimum wage in your state. You should be making at least that much per hour, but since you are running your own show, you can also make it a bit more. For the sake of simplicity, let's say that you decide that your time is worth $10

The Tip Jar TIPS

Phone It In

If you want to make your finances easier to track, sign up for cell phone access to your company bank account. You can usually just register for this access online, and it enables you to check your balance, ensure that payments went through, and even get pinged when your balance drops below a certain point. Such a notification helps if, say, you are out shopping for supplies and want to see if you have enough funds to buy an expensive item without having to log on or stop by the bank. Make sure, however, that you aren't using up minutes, texts, or web time on your cell phone that are outside of your paid plan, or the convenience could cost you more than it's worth.

an hour (before income tax). Add that to your production costs, which are $5, and you discover that need to charge at least $15 per dozen to make your company work for you.

Decide how much you want to make per hour of your time spent working. ▤

✸ **Competitors.** Next you need to look at what other local cupcake bakers are selling and for how much. You can do this by checking out their websites, stopping by and looking at the menu at a larger shop, or even calling and posing as a possible customer. Let's say the grocery store bakery charges $18 a dozen, and the gourmet shop downtown charges $24. Where do you fit in? Do you want to attract customers by undercutting your competitors with tasty, no-frills cupcakes that are perfect for kids' parties? Or do you want to out-do the fancy places and concoct new flavors and vegan options that can command big bucks? Once you know what sets you apart from your competitors, you can decide how much you should charge to add value to your service. If you think that charging a low price of $15 a dozen will help you sell more cupcakes and therefore make more cash in the long run, perhaps promoting yourself as the cheap baker in town is your niche (your profit: $15 – $5 = $10/hour). If you want to tap a luxury market that's willing to pay more for things they really want, perhaps high-end cupcakes priced at $30 per dozen are more your speed. Though you'll likely sell fewer cupcakes, you'll make more on each dozen you *do* sell (your profit: $30 – $5 = $25/hour).

Check out your competitors and write down what they charge. ▤ Then work out how you want to position your company among them. Then take into consideration all of the issues in this section—financial goals, expenses, time value, and competitors—and decide what your prices will be and write them down. Remember, these numbers aren't set in stone—they can always change.

Should You Publicize Your Prices?

Once you've set your prices, you need to decide how to let potential customers know about them. Some business owners publicize their prices, while others evaluate them according to the needs of each client. Which one you choose depends on the type of business you are running. If you're babysitting, it makes sense to tell people how much you charge upfront; for example, $10 per hour for the first kid, $5 per hour for each additional kid, $30 minimum per job. But if you run a website design company, every project you do will be very different. Even if you charge per page, there's a huge difference in the amount of work that goes into creating a simple HTML page and one with Flash and embedded videos. In that case, you can just announce that you create personalized quotes for each project and maybe set a minimum rate of $200 per project so people can see how your prices stack up against the competition. If you do this, it is still a good idea to figure out what each type of job is worth and keep it private. Then you can easily create your price quotes when the need arises.

Here are the pros and cons of each pricing method.

OPTION	THE PROS	THE CONS
Post a price list	You calculate prices once and move on. Also, if it's an easy job, you stand to make more money per hour than you thought you would.	You might not make enough money if a project is huge. For example, if you post that you charge $20 to mow a front yard, but someone hires you to cut a 10-acre yard, you will be mowing for hours without making much money. (You could get around this problem by being more specific with your lawn sizes.)
Offer price quotes	You will always charge a different (and fair for you) amount for each job based on the amount of work.	You have to do a little bit of work to provide a quote for each project. So if someone calls with a 10-acre lawn, you need to figure out how much you will charge, rather than referring to an established price list.

> *Don't ever let anyone tell you you're too young when you're raising money—just push harder. Create a clear plan and proof of your business concept and make sure you have a revenue model. Then present your idea as if you're 25. People will take you seriously.*
>
> —Chelsea Rustrum, founded web aggregation company Free Mania at age 14

Don't Blow That First Check!

By now, you're probably ecstatic about the thought of making all that glorious money. Just know that starting a business from scratch can often mean you have to work for awhile before you see a profit—especially if you received a loan that you need to pay back ASAP. Yeah, you want to buy a car right *now*, but it takes money to make money, and reinvesting the funds you make on your first few jobs will set you up to make even more cash (and buy an even hotter car) later. So take a deep breath every time you're tempted to run to the mall with your latest payment and remember that each dollar you save is an investment in your future.

Bank on It

Once you start raking in the cash, you need a place to put it, and no, under your mattress doesn't count. You might already have a savings account that your parents set up for you years ago, but you should definitely set up a separate account where you keep the business' money. It can either be a personal account with your name on it or a business account with your company name on it if you've already completed your registration stuff. Your bank will help you determine which works for your company. Your best bet is to ask your parents to take you to their bank; they already have a relationship there, which could help you avoid some potential fees associated with opening a new account.

Whatever type of account you open, it's important to keep your business funds separate from your regular money. This account should contain only the money you use to run your business, so if you pay folks, do it out of this account. And when you finally make enough to pay yourself, remove the money and put it in your own account so you can always see exactly how much money you have left to operate your business. Also, you won't be tempted to use company money to buy a slice after school.

Keep Track

It's important to establish a system for keeping track of your money so that you know how much you're making at any given time and, conversely, how much you have available to run your company. It would suck to promise to fill an order for 30 custom T-shirts, only to realize that you don't have enough money to buy the supplies.

Lucky for you, the internet makes managing your money super easy. Most banks nowadays offer free online access to your bank account so you can see your balance, tally all the money you've spent each month, and pay for your expenses right there on the bank's website. If you want something tailored more toward managing a business, you can pay to set up an account at Indinero.com, a site developed by a teen entrepreneur that links to your bank account and helps you handle all your accounting. It's like having an electronic accountant that alerts you *before* you accept the job when your cash flow is too low to purchase those supplies. Decide how you will keep track of your finances and write it down.

However you choose to do it, keep close track of your income (the money you make) and your expenditures (the money you spend to run your business). That way, you can see if the numbers you calculated when you started are really accurate or if things are changing as the economy and your business volume

> *To be competitive, you don't have to make the cheapest homemade soap out there. If your ingredients are better quality for people who have sensitive skin, that can be your edge.*
>
> – *Crystal Yan, founded book project* What's Next: 25 Big Ideas from Gen-Yers Under 25 *at age 17*

change. For example, let's say your research showed that it would cost $5 to bake and deliver a dozen of those cupcakes. But when you look at your expenditures, you realize that it's actually costing you an extra dollar because the price of milk went up last month, so you're making less profit. You then have the info you need to make a choice: Do you keep the prices the same and make a dollar less, increase your prices, or look for another, cheaper place to buy your milk? If you weren't keeping track of your money, you would have never known that you weren't banking as much profit as you thought you were.

How I Started My Business

We did a survey and found that, 8 to 1, people still prefer shopping at their local stores over shopping on the internet. But they were spending hours calling around to stores or, even worse, driving around to find out what each store had in stock. I thought people should be able to find local products in seconds using data on the internet. So we contacted locals stores, compiled their data, and created Milo.com. It searches the shelves of stores near you in real time to find the products you want at your local stores. We've been called the anti-Amazon because we use the internet to help people shop in real, local stores.

— Jack Abraham founded online product locator Milo.com at age 21

Resources

Business.gov/finance
This site provides info on insurance and business financing and has links to tons of small business grant and loan programs.

Grants.gov
Head here to find and apply for government-sponsored grant programs.

AccionUSA.org
This is the place for microfinancing, a practice in which regular people all over the country who believe in your idea lend you small amounts of money to get your business started.

Indinero.com
This low-cost site helps you manage your finances online.

NFTE.com
The Network for Teaching Entrepreneurship is a group of people committed to teaching entrepreneurship to young adults from low-income communities to help them succeed in life. Check out the site for info on programs and grant competitions.

SBA.gov/financialassistance
Visit this part of the U.S. Small Business Association's site to find great financial resources.

Rich Dad Poor Dad for Teens: The Secrets About Money—That You Don't Learn in School! **by Robert T. Kiyosaki and Sharon L. Lechter**
This book is an excellent source of advice about developing a positive relationship toward money and tips on how to manage it.

CHAPTER 6

WHO'S THE BOSS?

How to Hire and Manage a Crew

As you get deeper into planning your business, you'll start to get a better understanding of what it will take to run it, and you might realize that you need a staff. Think about all the places you like to spend your money: that gaming website, your favorite restaurant, the spot that sells those perfectly faded jeans. They all have some kind of staffing structure. For example, that gaming site you love might be just one guy sitting at his laptop all day and night, programming games and answering complaint emails. But your fave restaurant is being run by an owner, a manager, and an assistant manager as well as cooks, a hostess, and a clean-up crew. If you decide that you need a staff to help you pull things off, now is the time to figure out who you will bring on board and how you will manage them.

What Positions Are Needed?

So you need a staff. That means you need to figure out how many people will work for you, what their roles will be, and who will take orders from whom. (This is called establishing your company's staffing structure.) For example, say you have a house cleaning service: You might need someone who cleans with you, someone to create your website, and someone to design flyers and put them in mailboxes in your neighborhood. Or if you have a babysitting company, you might call the five most reliable sitters at your school and convince them to pool their efforts so you can all make more money.

While you're at it, come up with titles for everyone, including yourself. For instance, if you are doing all the baking for your cookie company, you might be the founder and head baker. Your friend who delivers the cookies could be called the director of delivery services. Note that some of the positions will be filled by actual staffers who you work with every day and are on the company's payroll, while other jobs may be done by contractors. Contractors are people who you hire to work on one project at a time, but they're not on the regular staff. For example, rather than hiring someone to work on promoting your business all the time, maybe you can pay someone to work on projects as you need them.

> *In a very small team, make sure you hire people who compensate for your weaknesses. I am not a software engineer, so that was the first employee we hired. And you have to be conservative at the beginning and look at it from a cash perspective: How much money do you have, and what's the cost of development?*
>
> *–Jeff Berger, founded employee recruiting portal KODA at age 22*

Write down the staff and contract positions you need to fill to make your business happen and create a title and job description for each position.

Who Will You Hire?

OK, you've created the slots that need to be filled. Whom do you know who can do the work? You'll probably want to look to your family and friends first because they will be eager to support your new endeavor. Is your brother a whiz at creating websites? Hire him as a contractor. Is your lab partner the most organized person you've ever met? Maybe she's perfect to schedule your tutoring appointments.

But it's also important to go beyond skill when filling positions. You need folks who will work for cheap (maybe even for free in the beginning, before the company starts making money) *and* who are diligent and dependable. So your friend who consistently does last night's homework on the bus on the way to school? Not so much. Look to your friends whom you can count on in a clutch and have time to spare. If you can't fill all the positions from within

The Tip Jar

Schedule It!

If you have employees who work various shifts or jobs, put together a master schedule that outlines everyone's responsibilities. Then post it online on a place like Google Docs and give everyone access. That way an employee doesn't have to text you every time he forgets his schedule— he can just log in. You could also use a master schedule like this to communicate changes with each other. But there should be some parameters around switching up the schedule. It's not cool to put someone on the schedule at the last minute and expect her to work. And an employee shouldn't be allowed to just post a note that says she has a wedding to attend right before she's supposed to work.

your circle, ask around your school and post requests on your social networking profiles. Have some ideas for employees? Write down their names next to the positions that they're perfect for. 📓

Working With Family and Friends

Most new businesses are started with the help of the people you're closest to—your family and your friends. But managing the people you love can be an excellent recipe for drama. The following tips can help you keep the love flowing.

✸ **Outline your expectations early.** If you tell your employees exactly what you need them to do, your sister can never say she "didn't know" it wasn't OK to order pay-per-view movies while cleaning a client's home or that being late to run an errand for the old lady at the end of the block isn't cool. Laying down the law in the beginning makes it easier for you to nip problems in the bud.

✸ **Manage those expectations.** It's a hard fact to face, but your friends and family just might suck a little. Why? It's not that they don't want you to do well, but this is *your* dream, not

> *When hiring friends or family, it is important to make sure that they are as committed to building the business as you are. And let them know upfront that, while you'll always be friends or family, business will always be business. If you go in with that understanding, you can avoid a lot of problems down the line.*
>
> *— Jack Abraham, founded online product locater Milo.com at age 22*

theirs, so you can never expect them to care (or to work) quite as much as you do. Plus they have other responsibilities, too. So be realistic about how much you can ask from them, and let them know *exactly* what you expect before they join the team. If someone doesn't do things the way you need them to, put yourself in their sneakers and go over what happened. Did you not give them clear instructions? Is it possible that they don't understand why it's important? Are they maybe just over working for you? If you decide you'd rather have someone as a friend than an employee, just say so—then go hang out!

❋ **Keep business and pleasure separate.** Yes, you and your buddies can have marathon conversations about how hard school is this year or how crazy your parents are, but when you're working together, it's important to draw a line between being their friend and being their boss. If you set clear boundaries, you will avoid situations where they get too comfortable with you and start thinking it's OK to halfway do their jobs because you're so cool with everything.

❋ **Never take them for granted.** It might be hard to believe, but no matter how dearly your dad and BFF love you, they do not *have* to work on your dream. So don't treat them like they owe you something. Always acknowledge when they do good work and express your gratitude for their help.

❋ **Don't play favorites.** Eventually, you might have people working for you who are not in your immediate circle. It's important that you don't treat them any differently than you treat the people who have been there for you all along. It'll just make the new folks resent the old ones and might make the old ones think they can get away with being lazy. Treat everyone the same, and you'll have fewer problems.

❋ **Learn how to let people go.** If a situation isn't working out, let your friend know that you think it's not a good fit for the business—or for her. After all, if she's slacking, she'd probably rather be doing something else with her time. If you make it neutral, it won't feel like a rejection. And do it before you get overly frustrated with her behavior. You can replace an employee, but good friends are a lot harder to come by.

Why Should People Work for You?

Now that you've established what you want your potential employees and partners to bring to the table, it's time to figure out what *you* have to offer *them*. Apart from money, which we'll get to on the next page, you need to create an environment where people actually want to work. If you can offer a top-notch service or product and be a good, confident leader, you'll have more luck employing people. It's important to make it look like you know what you're doing, even when you're not quite sure! On the flip side, don't be too proud to ask your employees for input and help. If you value their opinions, they are more likely to value yours. It's also key to maintain a regular, realistic schedule that doesn't infringe too much on their lives—your company is supposed to make the world better, not crankier. Finally, learn to be a good peacemaker and problem solver. Whether you're settling a dispute between employees or defending their work to an enraged client, they need to know that you'll work toward solutions that have their best interests at heart.

Keeping Things Creative

You can move your business forward by creating an environment that encourages new ideas. It's one thing to tell your employees that you welcome their ideas, and it's quite another to show them every day. Make idea generation time a regular part of your business process.

> *It's important to surround yourself with positive people who are trying to be successful themselves. That way you'll have other people around who understand what you're going through. It just feels better to be around people like that.*
>
> *—Tevyn Cole, founded clothing design company School Me at age 10*

How I Started My Business

I run a development company that creates and hosts websites. It started as a hobby. I was building websites for myself and I really enjoyed selling and marketing them and just getting them out there, and it just grew from that. Once I realized that it was profitable, that I could actually make a living out of it, I got serious.

—Donny Ouyang, founded website development and marketing company Kinksaro Tech Limited at age 13

Hold monthly (or every-other-month) staff meetings where you ask everyone to come up with one new idea and allow no judgment of those ideas. The results could be amazing. Maybe someone has a recipe for a new marshmallow peanut butter cookie or an idea to fix bicycles for free at the annual charity bike race so you can promote your service to the town's most die-hard bike riders. Your company can only benefit when you allow creative juices to flow.

Paying People

Though you may be one someday, you're not a billionaire mogul just yet. That means paying folks will be a little rough, especially when you're first starting out. But that's one of the benefits of working with people who care about you: They are usually willing to negotiate. Whether you give them a cut for each lawn they help you mow or cookies from each batch they package, here's betting all the rainbow sprinkles in the pantry that they will pitch in with your business if you ask them nicely. And consider bartering; you could offer your brother a free closet cleaning in exchange for a website design. Just be consistent: You can't give your brother cash for cutting lawns and pay your sister in laundry duty (unless she specifically asks for it, of course).

That being said, if you want your business to be legit, you should have a goal of paying all of your employees once you start making money. Whether family member or friend, no one wants to work for free forever.

When considering salaries, it's important to pay fairly; if your workers find out that you're charging clients $50 an hour to paint their houses but you're only paying them $5, they're not going to be your workers for much longer. And you have to pay them the right way, too. Think about how your parents get paid: If they work full time for a company, they bring home paychecks at regular intervals, whether it's every week, every other Friday, or on the first and the fifteenth of the month. That's a good thing—knowing when they're going to get the money they earned allows them to make plans and to pay bills. Things are no different when it comes to paying your employees. Whether you pay your friends a percentage of your fee each time they help you assemble furniture or give them a weekly paycheck, it's important that they know exactly what they should expect when it comes to their money. Would you work for someone who just paid you whenever they felt like it? Didn't think so. You created your budget in Chapter 5, so it should be easy now to figure out exactly how much you will pay the folks who work for you. Write down how and when you will pay your employees and contractors.

> *When figuring out how much to pay people, it's generally important to figure out what the market rate is and use that as a starting point. Also, people may prefer things like stock compensation to cash compensation, so it's not always about pay. We've found that people who are invested in the company's future are more productive employees.*
>
> *- Jack Abraham, founded online product locater Milo.com at age 22*

How I Started My Business

I was grounded and furious with my parents. I saw my dad reading a parenting book that gave him the worst advice! It was then that I realized that parenting advice was not complete. Parents needed kids' insight. I started interviewing teens to write my first book, You're Grounded!, which advised adults how to parent from a teen point of view. I self-published it at 17 and distributed paperback copies. But I wanted to expand the project into a company that would provide advice to parents from teens' perspectives in the form of websites, blogs, webinars, books, and events. So I saved money throughout college to do this, mostly by babysitting, and I made it all happen by the time I was 22. Today, our company is widely known and employs 121 teen interns who write and share advice with parents!

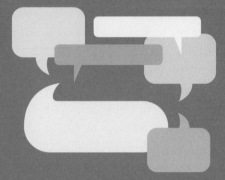

—Vanessa Van Patten, founded teen-run parenting advice company Radical Parenting at age 16

Quiz! What Kind of Boss Are You?

One of the best things about being an entrepreneur is that you're the boss and you call all the shots. But that means you need to develop good management skills in order for your company to be successul. Take this quiz to find out your natural boss style—and how you can improve upon it.

1. **The new student in your homeroom is kinda hot. You:**

a. Pounce at the bell, making yourself available for lunch today—and a date tomorrow night.

b. Want to say hi, but you know your best friend will want first crack, so you keep moving.

c. Think about going over, but remember that you left your book for next period in your locker and have to run to get it.

d. Sprint over and run down an exhaustive list of dos and don'ts for making a good impression at your school (which you've prepared for just this situation).

e. Introduce yourself and offer an escort to first period.

2. **Your parents are out of town for the weekend, and you're in charge of your little bro. You:**

a. Lock him in his room. You'd rather not worry about him this weekend.

b. Get talked into carting him and his awful friends around all day.

c. Plan to take him to the park and the planetarium and the zoo—but never get around to leaving the house.

d. Make him go over his homework with you on Friday and watch him clean his room on Saturday so you can make sure that he doesn't just shove everything under the bed.

e. Send him out with his buddies, then let him tag along at tonight's killer party.

3. **You're seven years old again, and you just got your allowance! You:**

a. Buy yourself a popsicle, some chips, and some candy, then eat them in front of your little sister. She should have hustled up her own money.

b. Buy treats for all your friends. Who cares if you only got a piece of gum?

c. Buy Kool-Aid and popsicle sticks from the dollar store to make your own treats but forget to put them in the freezer.

d. Ask for a bomb pop but only if it has the red part on the top, the white part in the middle, and the blue on the bottom.

e. Buy popsicles for your little sister and yourself, then put the rest in your piggy bank.

4. **Which of these words best describes you?**

a. Outgoing!

b. Shy.

c. Unique.

d. Exact.

e. Calm.

5. **Your sworn frenemy posts a snarky comment on your wall. You:**

a. Delete it and go to her house. You're taking this to the streets.

b. Delete it and yell at her—through your computer screen.

c. Start to send her a message but get distracted by an incoming text.

d. Leave it and point out all the things that were wrong with her comment, including the spelling mistakes.

e. Delete it and tag her in that picture you have of her picking her nose. Payback sucks.

6. **Your geography teacher assigned groups for your latest project. You:**

a. Take the lead; you already have a fab plan.

b. Sit back; somebody else will run the show.

c. Have a million ideas for what you could do. Now to narrow it down to just one....

d. Tell everyone exactly what they will contribute to the mix.

e. Ask everyone what they think and then suggest a vote to pick the best idea.

7. **It's your first date with that special someone. You:**

a. Veto all activity suggestions. You want to show off your bowling skills!

b. Let your date plan the night.

c. Try to cram your first three dates into one: Who wouldn't like to go swimming, kart racing, and skating all in one night?

d. Tell your date to be ready at 7:33 and to wear that outfit you like.

e. Ask if your date has an activity in mind, then pick a restaurant for dessert.

8. **Your idea of a good time with your friends is:**

a. Something you planned that you're not sure they'll like but you know will be good for them.

b. Whatever they want to do; you're easy.

c. Spending a whole, jam-packed day together.

d. Dinner reservations at 6, a concert (fifth row, centerstage tickets) at 8, and chocolate ice cream at 11.

e. Something you worked out together while texting.

9. **Your business is up and running. You asked your right-hand friend to follow up on a customer service issue. He didn't. You:**

a. Fire him.

b. Do it yourself. He must have had a good reason for not doing it.

c. Tell him that's unacceptable, then run a new idea you have by him.

d. Knew that he wouldn't do it, so you handled it before the customer could complain.

e. Ask him why, then have him fix it.

10. **When meeting new people, you:**

a. Jump in, dominating the convo with your witty observations.

b. Hang back; if they want to get to know you, they'll come over.

c. Tell them a million things about your life.

d. Ask a million questions about their lives.

e. Listen a little, talk a little. You love learning what makes other people tick.

If you got mostly As, you're ...
The Tough Stuff Boss

Whether you're at school or on a date, you know how to get things done. That's a great trait to have as an entrepreneur. Whether your goal is to lock down the tri-state area or to be a billionaire with locations around the globe, it will serve you well. The thing is, you have a tendency to steamroll folks and dismiss their ideas. That might work when dealing with your annoying little sister or a mean customer, but when it comes to running a business, you could miss out on great opportunities and alienate your workers. And people who hate you don't make good employees. Try asking what others think sometimes and incorporate the best ideas. You'll make them feel like a real part of the empire you're building, and that means they'll work extra hard for you because they *want* to—not because they're afraid of what you'll do if they don't.

If you got mostly Bs, you're ...
The Great Friend Boss

"Go with the flow" is your motto, and your employees love that about you! They know that you'll understand if they can't work tonight, and you won't yell if they forgot to make a delivery because you are so nice to everyone. But you can be agreeable to a fault. It sucks, but it's true: People will often take advantage of you if they can, even your friends. So whether you're giving your BFF first crack at that hot new kid who you saw first or letting your employees walk all over you for the sake of keeping the peace, you're selling yourself short. Have confidence that what you think matters, and it'll radiate through all parts of your life. People are attracted to confidence, and your employees will respect you and work hard for you if you make it clear that what you say goes.

If you got mostly Cs, you're ...
The Mad Scientist Boss

Talk about creative; you don't just think outside the box, you think outside the circle, triangle, and octagon, too. You probably come up with new ideas while you're sleeping, don't you? Your buddies appreciate how different you are, and no matter what industry you work in, your skill at brainstorming will help move your business forward. But sometimes you get going on so many different ideas that none of them get enough attention to get off the ground. And the ideas that *do* make it beyond the planning stages often feel a bit scattered.

If you can train yourself to focus on just one project at a time, you'll accomplish a lot more.

If you got mostly Ds, you're …
The Micromanager Boss

You know the importance of doing things right the first time. Your attention to detail is unparalleled, and here's betting that no one in your life can think of a time when you've dropped the ball. Plus your buddies know that if you plan the evening, every moment of it is going to count. That ability to rock it every time will make your customers love you. But the same quality may make your employees loathe you. Your need for everything to be perfect means that you don't trust them to make any decisions or to do things their own way. That can feel stifling to employees who need a little more freedom. It's also bad because they'll start to only do things halfway, knowing that you're just going to follow behind them and fix their mistakes. Try to have a little more faith in their abilities, and take an afternoon off from time to time!

If you got mostly Es, you're …
The Collaborative Boss

Diplomatic, but firm; That's you. You're naturally adept at ruling with an iron fist without using it to crush those around you. While you *can* lead, you also know how and when to let others share the spotlight so they feel like valued members of your team. It's a skill that will serve you well when establishing expectations for your employees and managing them day to day. Just be careful that you don't take the collaboration *too* far. It's important to consider the input of others, but you shouldn't compromise so much that you don't follow your heart (or your gut). Your staff should know that you always have the final word on issues pertaining to the business. You are the boss after all.

Be Well Rounded

You may have found that you scored similarly for two of the categories. Some bosses are a combination of types. But even if you do have a predominant personality type as a boss, read the other types as well. Each one has great positive qualities that you can learn to cultivate and combine with your own natural abilities to make yourself the best boss ever!

Resources

Entrepreneur.com/humanresources
This section of Entrepreneur.com is all about hiring and managing your staff.

My Biggest Mistake ... and How I Fixed It: Lessons From The Entrepreneurial Front Lines
by Marcia Pledger
This book is full of real-life leadership advice from small business owners.

Understanding and Changing Your Management Style
by Robert C. Benfari
This is a book that will help you determine your management method and change it for the better.

> *It's really important to know what motivates people and to create a work environment that's condusive to creativity and happiness. It's also great to give people their own space in the work environment. We have a dog that runs around the office, and people seem to like that.*
>
> *— Jack Abraham, founded online product locater Milo.com at age 21*

CHAPTER 7

EXTRA, EXTRA

Telling the World About Your Big Idea

Imagine that your favorite television show started a new season. But there were no commercials or ads on the sides of buses so you didn't know about it. You'd be pretty upset, right? That's how all the folks in need of your delivery services or your errand running would feel if you didn't put the word out about your business. Not to mention that it would suck if you put all this effort into starting your company and no one ever came knocking. That's why it's so important to develop a marketing strategy: a plan that lays out how you're going to get people to buy what you're selling. Starting a business without one is like texting on a phone with no bars. No one is getting the message.

Stand Out to Get Ahead

The first step in developing your marketing plan is to establish what makes your product different from your competition's. Say you want to turn a buck off your amazing ability to rock math classes. Are there other tutoring businesses in your area? What will make yours different? Maybe another company is run by adults who haven't been in high school in years. You have an advantage because you aced ninth grade algebra last year and it's still fresh in your head. Or perhaps your prices will be lower so other teens can hire you themselves instead of going to their parents for funds. Knowing what makes you stand out will help you tell other folks why they should give *you* their hard-earned cash instead of the other guy. This is called your competitive edge. Apple built its very successful business just this way: by continuously finding ways to set itself apart from other computer companies. Brainstorm ways that your new business will be different from existing ones. 📓

Who Wants Some?

After you've figured out what makes your product or service different, it only makes sense to figure out who actually cares. It could be just one audience (group of people) or it could be several. These various audiences make up your market (all the people who might patronize your business). For example, if you have a tutoring company, one audience might be students at your school. Another might be their parents, and a third could be your teachers. In this case, you might already know a lot of your market. With other businesses, some people in your market might be strangers—but that doesn't mean you can't identify them. Say you fix computers. Your market could be classmates, your parents' friends, people in your neighborhood who own computers, and anyone one who finds your website while looking for someone to fix their laptop. Who wants to buy what you're selling? Make a list of potential audiences and explain why each one would want your product. 📓

Give the People What They Want—When You Can

After you figure out who might want to pay their hard-earned money for your service or product, you need to determine exactly what they want it to do for them. You probably have ideas about what makes your company different and new, but you might have to tweak them based upon what the market is actually looking for. For instance, perhaps your customers want your audio equipment rental to be cheaper than the shop downtown. Or maybe there is a real need in your area for web designers who are experts at using Flash. If so, you may want to consider setting your rental prices a little lower or learning Flash. That being said, make sure that you are not compromising your vision simply to please a few customers, especially if the point of starting your business was to live your passion through your work. Say you're a musician. If the market wants more bubblegum pop but you're punk to the core, you'll just have to learn to create your own market. Staying true to what you love is the only way to be genuinely successful.

Survey Says

The best way to learn what the market wants is simply to ask your potential customers if your product interests them. Take a survey: It can be as simple as calling your friends and asking if they'd pay you to train them at the gym. Or you could create an online form to see if any

> As an entrepreneur, you have to know when to listen and when not to. When I was just starting out, this older woman said my cards were "ghetto," because I used some slang in the text. It was horrible, but I'm really proud of myself for saying, "You know what, I'm not going to listen to that!" I refused to change my cards and turn this company into something I don't believe in because then it wouldn't be mine.
>
> —Chauncey Holloman, founded greeting card company Harlem Lyrics at age 17

of your social networking friends need someone to spice up their profiles. If you get a good response, you'll not only know who wants your service, you'll have some great feedback on how you can make it appeal to a wide range of people. There are several websites that make it easy to create surveys, send them out, and analyze data. Just search for one on the web.

Here are some sample survey questions you can modify to create your own.

* Do you currently use a _____(service or product)?

* Where do you go for your _____ (service or product)?

* How much do you pay for your current _____ (service or product)?

* What do you like about your _____ (service or product)?

* What would you change about your _____ (service or product)? Why?

* What would it take for you to switch to a new _____ (service or product)?

Analyzing Your Data

So you've surveyed everyone and have gotten some great information about how many people are dissatisfied with their kid's tutor and how much they'd be willing to pay for truly unique handmade necklaces. Maybe the feedback matches up perfectly with what you're already doing (offering longer sessions or charging $100 per necklace). More often than not, there will be a little bit of a disconnect between the way you plan to market your product and what your audience wants. Then you have a decision to make. If you think the info makes sense and will make your business better, you can decide to adapt accordingly. But if it will take you completely outside of your mission and your vision for yourself and your company, you might choose not to incorporate it into your overall plan. Either way, it's good information to have.

Where's the Party?

OK, now you know who your audiences are and what they want. But that means nothing if you don't know how to find them. Effective marketing is all about reaching people where they will best receive your message. Think about your favorite shows. Chances are, you know when they are coming on because you see ads for them on your favorite websites. Know why? Because marketers know that people who like quirky cartoon shows probably also like quirky websites, so they place ads on the sites you check every day.

You have to think the same way. If you want to promote your tutoring business to parents, you have to go where they are. Maybe that means asking to speak briefly at the next PTA meeting, passing out handbills as parents walk to their cars, posting flyers on bulletin boards, or running an ad in the local newspaper. (Some people *do* still read newspapers.) Whichever method you pick, just make sure that the message reaches the intended audience—you're probably not going to get many parent clients if you only hand out flyers at the skate park. Where do the people who want to use your business hang out? Write down every place you can think of, including advertising spaces and virtual gathering places, such as social networks and specific websites.

> *In a start-up, you are trying to promote your company on a shoestring budget. We found that the best way to do this was with partnerships. Look for organizations with common goals and ones that have the user base that you need. Companies that you might think of as being competitors may turn out to be your greatest partners. It never hurts to explore those opportunities.*
>
> *—Jeff Berger, founded employee recruiting portal KODA at age 22*

Paper Route

There are a million ways to reach people once you know where they are, but some of the most low-tech methods often yield the best results. Traditionally, word of mouth can make or break a business. It's the reason companies adopt "The customer is always right" policies: A satisfied customer will sing your praises to potential customers and bring you new business. It also works if noncustomers talk you up. Ask your parents to tell all their friends about your indie music zine, ask your granny to tell the ladies at her church that you run errands for a fee, and ask your older brother to talk up your moving business to all his friends who are transitioning into the dorms at the college across town.

Here are some other simple ways to get the word out.

* **Business cards.** It seems old school, but you need to be prepared to give out info about your business at all times; telling people to find you online is not good enough, especially when dealing with older clients. Include your company name, your name and title, a logo, and the URLs to your website and company social networking pages. Print them for free at VistaPrint.com. Just pay shipping.

* **Announcements.** Tell people about your company every chance you get. Make an announcement in your homeroom, put a notice in the school paper, get it in the church bulletin. Anywhere your audience might be, you should be as well.

* **Flyers.** Jump on your computer, pull up a word processing program, and go to work! A simple flyer can get the message across about your business clearly and succinctly. Large, eye-catching graphics are good, and you might want to create little phone number tags at the bottom so people can take one without pulling down your whole flyer. Post them wherever your audience spends time, but check your local flyer distribution laws and get permission if necessary.

* **Handbills.** These are just like flyers, only smaller. Just shrink your flyer so that you can fit four on a page. Then cut them out and hand them to people at events and on the street.

* **Mailers.** These are basically flyers that you mail to a list of potential customers. VistaPrint can help you with both printing and compiling a list.

Brainstorm low-tech methods that you think will help you sell your business and write them down. ▣ Then ask for any help you need to make them happen.

Go Digital

Of course, you also want to tap into your market via the internet. Here are a few high-tech marketing methods to consider.

✳ **Create a website.** Nowadays, companies don't seem legit if they don't have a web presence. Plus a site provides interested customers a central place to go to find out about your business. Creating a website is actually pretty easy. If you read Chapter 4, you may have already bought a domain name. After doing this, come up with a design plan. You can start from scratch if you or a friend have the skills to make it happen. If not, Google "website templates" and pick one that best reflects your company; you can add your logo to customize it. Squarespace.com and Intuit.com both make it cheap and easy to create a website. They even offer free trials before a small monthly subscription fee kicks in. Remember that your site

The Tip Jar

Multitask

Promote your business while you're doing other stuff. Add a signature to your personal and business email accounts that talks up your business, features your logo, and links to your website. That way, every email you send gets the word out. While you're at it, set up your website so that it updates to Twitter and Facebook every time you add stuff so you can promote without even thinking about it (check with your website hosting company for help). Multitask offline by putting stickers and magnets of your company logo on your book covers and car so you'll be a moving billboard; T-shirts and hats serve the same purpose.

> *We focus a lot of effort on search engine optimization. This is free if you know how to do it, and coming up at the top of Google is invaluable for getting new readers and customers. We spend no money on paid advertising. We would rather put our time into getting free media spots.*
>
> — *Vanessa Van Patten, founded teen-run parenting advice company Radical Parenting at age 16*

Be sure to use words on your site that are typically associated with your industry (that's your particular type of business) so when people do online searches, your company's page will pop up. For example, if you repair computers, use words and phrases like "computers," "repair," "crash," "virus," "hard drive," and "memory." This is called search engine optimization (SEO), and it's a great way to increase your presence on the internet. There are entire companies that just focus on SEO, so if you're interested in learning more about this, read up on the subject online.

✿ **Write a blog.** If you run a company that customers might be interested in reading about, a blog could help you make a personal connection with your audience and therefore sell more product. For instance, if you make art out of found objects, you might talk about the latest materials you came upon and the places where you found them. Try Blogger.com or WordPress .com for free blog templates that you can add to your website.

✿ **Make a virtual storefront.** You can make a lot more sales if people can just whip out their credit cards and buy. For instance, if you sell any type of homemade craft (greeting cards, headbands, bracelets), think about creating a storefront on Etsy .com. It's free to create a customizable page, and you only pay a fee when you sell an item. If music is your thing, there are tons of sites out there that help musicians sell their tracks online; just do a quick search. But if you sell products online, the most important thing is to have a plan for fulfilling orders. You need to have enough raw materials on hand to create items, and you must figure out the most cost-effective way to ship *before* you make a sale (see "Growing Your Business" on page 142 for more on this topic).

✹ **Work your (social) network.** Create profiles and fan pages specifically for your company—don't use your personal ones—and ask your friends and customers to write testimonials on them about how much they like your business. (They should do this on your company website, too.) And don't forget to comment on other pages; people will be more likely to comment on yours if you share the love. When it comes to sending messages to your followers, friends, or fans, be sure to only send them when you really have something interesting and important to say. You don't want them to get annoyed and unfriend your business!

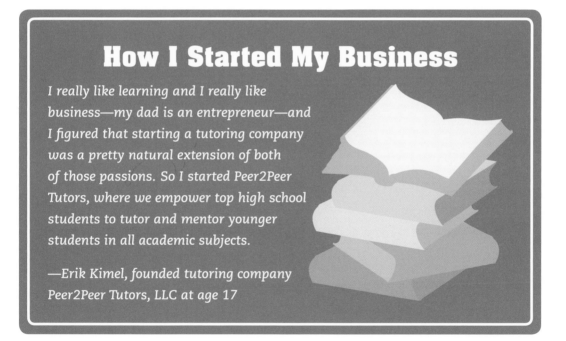

How I Started My Business

I really like learning and I really like business—my dad is an entrepreneur—and I figured that starting a tutoring company was a pretty natural extension of both of those passions. So I started Peer2Peer Tutors, where we empower top high school students to tutor and mentor younger students in all academic subjects.

—Erik Kimel, founded tutoring company Peer2Peer Tutors, LLC at age 17

✸ **Help customers find you.** Set up free profiles for your business on search engines and listings websites such as Yelp.com, Google.com, Local.Yahoo.com, YellowPages.com, AngiesList.com, and MerchantCircle .com. A listing for your product or service on Craigslist can win you business, too.

What high-tech methods can you use to get the word out about your company? Write down things to try.

Speak Up!

Once you know who you want to sell to and how you're going to reach them, it's important to know what you're going to say to them. As the head of your company, it's your job to be able to express what you do so that others can understand it easily. You need to create an elevator pitch, which is a short paragraph that says who you are, what your company does, and what makes it different—all in the time it would take for a typical elevator ride. Here's a sample elevator pitch that you can use to model your own:

"Hi, my name is Patty, and I own Picture Perfect Photography. We take amazing photos of special moments. Our services include family portraits, first birthday party pictures, and wedding photography.

The Tip Jar TIPS

Practice Makes Perfect

A well-written elevator pitch is a great tool for explaining your business to potential clients. But while it's easy to ramble on for ages about what makes your company awesome and worthy of others' time and money, boiling down all your greatness into a 30-second speech requires some real skill. Get the most out of your pitch by honing in on one main concept, such as "I upgrade computer systems in two hours or less" or "I run the only delivery service for sick people in the tri-state area." Then build a couple of sentences around that. Test drive it on your grandma and your little cousin. If *they* understand precisely what you do, you're ready for prime time!

We're versatile and can shoot in all digital and film formats, and our prices are guaranteed to beat out competitors. I'd love to talk to you about how we can do business together."

Got an idea for your own elevator pitch? Write it down and work on it until it sounds perfect. 🖹 Then practice it out loud, using your group of advisors as your guinea pigs.

Party Time

Another way to get the word out about your company is to have an event or to take part in one that's already happening. If your town holds a fair every summer, you could get a booth and show off your card designs or ask your friends to let you cut their hair in a live demonstration. Want to walk pets for a living? Get permission from your city to set up a table at the local dog park—you can play music, toss out pet treats (if owners say

it's OK), and pass out coupons for $5 off their first walk. Anything that puts you out in front of potential customers is a good thing; the more people who know what you're doing, the better your chances of snagging new customers.

Stop the Presses

Another way to tell people about what you're doing is to get newspapers, magazines, and television shows to do the work for you. If you have something newsworthy going on (something bigger than introducing a new cookie flavor), you might be able to get coverage. The best way to inform local news outlets about what you're doing is to send them a press release. Send it to the appropriate email address from the outlet's "Contact Us" page.

It's almost impossible to move forward if you don't network. In the beginning, I was really nervous about walking up to people I didn't know. Over the years it started to come naturally, and I now feel more comfortable introducing myself.

—Tevyn Cole, founded clothing design
company School Me at age 10

Here's a sample press release that you can use to create your own.

Contact: FOR IMMEDIATE RELEASE
Ellen Wright
555-555-5555
ellen.wright@tjstees.com
www.tjstees.com
August 27, 2010

TJ'S T-SHIRT DESIGNS OFFERS FREE CLOTHES
TO FAMILY WHO LOST ALL IN FIRE

CLEVELAND, OHIO—Today, TJ's T-Shirt Design, a local custom casual wear company, donated a large package of clothing to the Farmer family, who lost their home in an electrical fire yesterday. The donation came just a week before the start of the new school year.

"I was so sad to hear about what happened," says TJ Wright, the 17-year-old CEO of the company. "I knew we had to do something. I just hope this small gift can give the Farmers one less thing to worry about."

The family is grateful for the clothing, which not only includes designer T-shirts but denim jeans as well. "You never expect something like this to happen, but we've been so lucky to have people rally around us," says Frankie Farmer, who has temporarily moved his family into his cousin's home downtown.

If you have something you'd like to contribute to the Farmers, TJ's is collecting items for the family; just drop them off at the company's 555 Main Street location.

TJ's T-Shirt Designs was founded in 2009 to give teenagers unique, high-quality, low-cost clothing that they won't see on everyone else.

Resources

VistaPrint.com
This site lets you design and print your own business cards for free; you just have to let them put their (tiny) logo on the back of your cards.

Intuit.com/free-website-builder
This site offers industry-specific, customizable website templates. There's a free trial, but you'll have to pay after the first month.

Google.com/addurl
This is where you let Google know that your website exists.

Bing.com/webmaster
Go here to add your site to Microsoft's Bing search engine.

SurveyMonkey.com
Visit this site to create and send free surveys to people. You can use them to see what your potential audiences think about your business.

Zoomerang.com
This survey creation site lets you ask millions of random people how they feel about your business concept so you can put their feedback to work for you.

Blogger.com
Put the power of blogging at your fingertips for nada.

WordPress.com
Another great site for free blog templates and tools, WordPress can get you blogging fast.

Etsy.com
Etsy is the premier place to sell handmade goods on the web.

CHAPTER 8

REPEAT BUSINESS

Customer Service Rules

Right about now, people are climbing over each other in an attempt to hand you their last dollar because your service or product is *that* good. But it's not enough to just get people in the door—you have to get them to come back. It's called *repeat* business. Sure, an excellent offering at an amazing price will excite your customers. But you can't discount the importance of great customer service. Think about it: There's this one chain of restaurants that makes the best burger you've ever tasted. And there are three locations near your house. But you always go to the one way over on Broadway Avenue. Why? Because the girl at the drive-through window always gets your order right, and they are never out of ketchup! *That* is great customer service. Do it right, and people will go out of their way to reach you, too.

Keep People Happy

When it comes to dealing with clients, it's true what they say: The customer is always right. That means that, even when things go wrong, you aim to avoid arguments with your customers and do whatever it takes to send them away happy. One approach to this is to think of how you'd like to be treated if you came to someone with the same grievance your customer has. So, for instance, if a new client says that you killed her plant while you were house sitting, even though you know it was dying when you got there, you might offer to buy her a new one anyway because that's what you'd want if you were in her shoes. And everyone who works for you should know this rule. You could be lovely and amazing to every one of your customers, but if one of your employees is rude on the phone when he books appointment for you to paint houses, he's leaving a bad taste in your customers' mouths. That could cause them to leave their money in their wallets.

Why bend over backward? Because one angry customer will always be louder than 10 satisfied ones. People tend to complain more than they compliment (sad, but true), so while a satisfied customer will tell a couple of her friends who are going on vacation that you were a very responsible house sitter, a disgruntled one will tell *everybody* that you suck—even if you don't. And websites like Yelp.com make it even easier for customers to review your business and to have their opinions (positive *or* negative) reach tons of people in an instant. It might be hard to accept it, but even if you have to drop $20 to replace the plant your customer says you killed while weeding her garden (and you only made $40 on the job to begin with), it'll help you come out ahead at the end of the day.

Of course, if a client is especially rude or threatens you, call your parents for backup and cut business ties with them. No amount of money is worth being treated like crap. Period.

What's in It for You?

It sounds like this customer service stuff is all for, um, customers. But it has some advantages for you, too.

Fun. Happy customers create a pleasant working environment for you; smiles are contagious. Besides, if you wanted to be angry at work all day, you would get a job at the mall.

Repeat business. When you meet the needs of your customers, they know that they can count on you to do it again. Why would they try that artist across town if they already know that your murals *and* your service are awesome?

Good word of mouth. Think about it: When you want to buy something online, you read reviews from people who've already bought it to see if they had a good experience. And if someone wrote on Facebook that the customer service reps sucked, you might look for another option. If you treat your customers well, it will pay off in positive reviews that attract others.

> *You can never win an argument with a customer. Ever. Something is going to happen, someone is not going to be happy, and you're going to think that you're right. But it doesn't matter. You have to provide excellent service, and that means giving the customer what they're looking for—even if you take a hit on it. You're reputation is worth more than that one transaction.*
>
> *—Erik Kimel, founded tutoring company Peer2Peer Tutors, LLC at age 17*

Top Five Best Practices

There are specific things you can do to make your customers feel appreciated and comfortable with your company, no matter what industry you're in. Here are the top five.

1 Smile. Whether you're communicating in person, on the phone, or via email, it'll come through and let them know that you're happy to be serving them.

2 Remember—and use—their names. It's the quickest way to show someone that you care about them and their specific concerns. If you're dealing with adults, use "Ms.," "Mrs.," and "Mr."

3 Say "please" and "thank you." You learned it in preschool—turns out it still works. Do it when customers hand you cash. Do it at the holidays with a nice card. In whatever way you can think of, just do it.

How I Started My Business

I love to eat and I've always liked baking, especially cookies. In the sixth grade, I made cookies for one of my friend's birthdays, and everybody liked them, so I started making them for special occasions. Eventually my mom was like, "You're not going to keep making free cookies for everybody—they cost money!" So I started selling them for fifty cents each. I wasn't making any money, so I increased my prices and things took off from there.

—Gabrielle McBay, founded cookie company Crumbs by Gabrielle at age 13

4 If a customer has a concern, repeat it back to him. It'll help you to clarify the problem and show him that you care enough to get it right.

5 Apologize when something goes wrong, even if nobody complains, and even if it wasn't your fault. Your customers will appreciate it.

About Etiquette

One of the disadvantages of starting a company as a teen is that some people might not take you seriously simply because of your age. That means it's even more important for you to practice proper business etiquette than it is for an older tycoon. There are some things you should practice no matter how you're communicating with clients, potential customers, and investors. Absolutely no swearing! And never, ever use slang when dealing with adults, even if they use it first. (If your client base is primarily other teens, it's OK to use it with them.) Also, you should be polite in all situations, even if someone is being less than polite with you. Being the bigger person is always professional.

There are a few areas where you should take special care when dealing with clients.

The Tip Jar

Be Prepared

Keeping complete, accurate records can help to protect you in the event of customer service issues. If some crazy customer tries to get out of paying you because of some so-called late delivery, you can pull up the receipt her husband signed when you dropped off her repaired computer last week. You can buy a receipt book that creates carbon copies of everything you write in it or use money management software to quickly create, email, or print detailed, customized receipts for jobs.

❋ **Phone conversations.** The biggest thing to remember about talking on the phone is that it's actually a great tool. So often, we think it's easier to shoot out a quick email than to pick up the phone, but sometimes the best way to connect with a customer is to provide the personal touch of a call.

* **Face-to-face meetings.** Here your appearance really matters. You don't have to throw on a three-piece suit, but what you do wear should be clean, ironed, and free of holes and stains. That means you should leave your favorite concert tee and ripped jeans on the floor of your closet—they're probably dirty anyway.

* **Email.** When it comes to sending email messages, keep it simple. First, pick a straightforward address. Your first initial and last name @whatever.com is a good look. When it comes to writing messages, skip the smiley faces and exclamation points (they can come across as childish or unprofessional), and keep in mind that using all caps is the equivalent of shouting in cyberspace. Also: Remember all those proper greetings you learned during your elementary school lessons on how to write a letter? Use them. Email can be a bit more casual, so it's OK to just say "Hello Mr. Soandso" at the top of your email, but definitely use an opening greeting. And sign off with "Sincerely," at the end. It's also a good idea to create an email signature (as mentioned on page 105) that will be

added to the end of each email you send so that your contact info will always be easily accessible. It should include your full name, your title, the name of your company, your email address, phone number, and company website.

* **Other online communications.** When communicating via your company's social networking pages, the same rules apply. Be conversational, but skip inappropriate language. Also, don't post videos or links that don't directly apply to your company; neither your love of body piercings nor your political views should creep onto the site profiles— they could cost you customers who disagree with your opinions. Remember, everything you post online will live there forever, so be careful what you put out there.

Ask How You're Doing

Another great way to be sure you're providing the best service possible is to simply ask. You might not always like what you hear, but customer feedback can be an effective tool in improving your business. There are a few ways to do it. You can ask customers how you did at the end of every transaction, but only the most vocal (or angry) folks will have much to say. A more effective way is to send them a survey after you provide a service or deliver a product, just like the ones you get after you buy something online. If your customers are older, it makes sense to leave them a paper survey with a stamped and addressed envelope so they can just drop it in the mail to you. For most people, however, you should be able to email them a survey, as discussed in Chapter 7; just ask for email addresses whenever you take orders. You can tie surveys directly to individual email addresses—so you'll know who said what—or make them anonymous, which might increase your chances of getting honest answers. Just tailor your questions to what you most need to know. Every business can benefit from feedback on its process—that's stuff like your customer service skills and how quickly you filled an order or completed a project. But if you sell a creative product or service, it might not help you much to ask questions about how customers loved the product. Art is a subjective thing, and hearing that a client wishes "you'd used a smidge more orange" in the painting you made won't help you run your business better. If customers only have great things to say, you'll know you're on the right track, and they'll be glad you cared enough to ask. If not, you'll likely learn a bunch about how you can improve your customer service. Either way, you win!

> *Surveys are so helpful to understand customer development. There are tons of online survey tools out there and most of these services offer free webinars on how to get started in designing a survey. You can even offer an incentive to people who take the survey, like an entry for a raffle of a free gift card. And be sure to ask for their contact info if you'd like to survey them again later.*
>
> —*Crystal Yan, founded book project* What's Next: 25 Big Ideas from Gen-Yers Under 25 *at age 17*

Change Can Be Good

Then comes the hard part: making changes based on the feedback. So if everyone says your brother is mean when he answers your company line, you'll need to have a difficult conversation with him about telephone etiquette. If he can't get it together, you might have to bring in someone else to replace him or your business could suffer. If half your customers confess that they think your red velvet cupcakes are a little, gulp, dry, you'll need to tinker with your recipe and have your advisors (taste testers!) help you bake a better product. You can do it—look how far you've already come. A little constructive criticism can make you more successful if you don't take it personally and let it inspire you to do better.

When the Going Gets Tough

No matter how hard you work at providing good customer service, someone is going to be dissatisfied at some point. The key is how you handle it. First, ask the client what you need to do to make him feel good about your interaction, and don't hesitate to

> *A teacher from my school asked me to fill a big hole in her yard. It was really serious stuff; I made her whole yard level again. We had agreed on a discounted price, but she didn't want to pay the balance even though her yard was beautiful and I had cleaned up things that had nothing to do with the hole. She nagged, whined, and cried about so much stuff—she even harassed some of my workers! I never got my money, but I learned then that all money is not good money. At some point you have to cut your losses.*
>
> *—Blaine Mickens, founded landscaping company Estate Groomers at age 14*

pick your advisors' brains if you need suggestions on how to make things right. Whether it's a refund or a redo, work with your client to make things better. If the problem involves the loss or damage of property (say, you ran over his favorite garden gnome with your riding mower), it's time to check your liability insurance and see if it can be handled that way.

If the customer still isn't happy, refund his money, offer your apologies for not meeting his expectations, and move on. If he posts negative reviews of your business online, ask your happier clients to counter-post with more positive, truthful reviews and keep moving. You can't win 'em all.

Resources

SurveyMonkey.com
This site—mentioned for surveying potential customers in Chapter 7—is also a good resource for collecting feedback from current customers.

Killer Customer Care: How to Provide Five Star Customer Service That Will Double and Triple Your Profits by George Colombo
A great read, this book will show you how to develop lasting relationships with customers.

Make It Glow: How to Build a Company Reputation for Human Goodness, Flawless Execution, and Being Best-in-class by Tom DeCotiis
This book is all about how to build a brand that customers will return to again and again.

A Complaint Is a Gift: Recovering Customer Loyalty When Things Go Wrong by Janelle Barlow and Claus Moller
Learn to turn negative feedback into customer satisfaction.

CHAPTER 9

DOING GOOD

Using Your Business to Improve the World

So far, we've talked about what running your own business can do for *you*. And that only makes sense; being an entrepreneur can provide independence, a creative outlet, and, of course, money. But one of the other amazing things about creating your own empire is that you can make *other* people's lives better, too. Some of the world's richest, most powerful business people do tremendous things for others. For instance, Bill Gates, the billionaire cofounder of Microsoft, started a charitable foundation in 1994 that has since given away more than $22 billion to aid health and reduce extreme poverty in developing countries and to improve high school education in America. But you don't have to be ridiculously rich to make a difference in the lives of others. Whether you use your cash, your influence, or just your time, your new company can be a vehicle to do a world of good.

How Can You Make a Difference?

There are a million little ways to give back to the community that supports you. Donating part of your company's proceeds is the obvious one, but there are a lot of other ways to do good. Each time you make a decision to treat your employees and vendors ethically or do something that honors and preserves the environment, you're using your powers for good. You can also choose to donate time to charity or start a mentoring program. Or you might come up with your own creative ways to save the world.

It Pays to Give Back

As with everything else to do with running a business, there are some tangible and intangible benefits to giving back.

✳ **You'll feel good.** You know that warm, fuzzy feeling you get when you help one of your grandma's friends clean her gutters on a Saturday afternoon instead of spending all your money at the mall? That's how you'll feel when you use your company to help others.

✳ **You'll create goodwill.** Doing for others is like doing for yourself. When you attach your company's name to a charity or help underprivileged people in your area, you help your business' reputation. When potential customers think about your company, they'll remember the great things you do and be more inclined to give you their money. Seriously.

✳ **It's financially viable.** Any money you give to charities with nonprofit

> *Just because you're young doesn't mean that you can't give away a lot of money. And just because you're not rich doesn't mean you can't give away a lot of money. I want to start a foundation and show people what is possible. Open your mind and enlarge the vision for your life.*
>
> —David Bridgeforth, founded public speaking and lifestyle coaching company Bridgeforth Communications at age 16

How I Started My Business

I was shopping for my best friend's birthday card and I realized that no greeting cards really catered to the teen market; they were all either way too mature or too kiddy. But rather than say, "Somebody should create this," I said, "I can do that!" So I decided to create a line of really niche-marketed greeting cards that would speak to teens, specifically African-Americans and hip-hop enthusiasts. I was adamant about doing this. And I also really wanted to create role models for African-American females. I went to my mom, and she said, "Give me a business plan."

—Chauncey Holloman, founded greeting card company Harlem Lyrics at age 17

status is tax deductible—so (depending on how much you give and how you file your taxes) it can actually *save* you money in the long run! Just keep accurate records of the amounts you give and the value of any products or services you donate so your accountant can factor it into your company tax returns.

❊ **It brings good luck.** Ever heard of karma? The word karma translates into "action" in the ancient language of Sanskrit, and it's a concept that has Buddhist and Hindu roots. The basic philosophy of karma is that good actions lead to good energy and bad actions lead to bad energy—or, as you may have heard in English,

"What goes around comes around." So when you run your business ethically—that is, in a way that is fair and moral—you're not only doing good, you're creating positive energy that will come back to you tenfold. And whether or not you buy into the theory of karma, you'll never go wrong by doing good.

Love Thy Employees

What better place to start all this ethics stuff than with the people who believe in you enough to work toward your dream? This is especially important for teenage entrepreneurs because many of your employees (if you have any) will likely be friends and family, and no relationship is worth ruining over business. Fostering free, open communication can go a long way when it comes to creating a positive work environment. Talk to your employees to find out how they think you're doing as a boss, and incorporate any good ideas they have for making your business an even better place to work. Some other ways to keep them happy include paying them a fair wage, paying them on time, expecting them to work reasonable hours (you can't fire your best friend because she refused to skip history class to make a delivery), and providing clean, comfortable working conditions (no, you can't build a sweatshop in your garage). Just keep in mind that treating your employees ethically doesn't mean that you shouldn't expect them to work hard for their money—it just means that you won't make them miserable while they do it.

This is something that I'm still working on because it's pretty difficult, but you should always listen to your employees' thoughts and ideas. And don't just tell them exactly what to do; let them have some freedom.

—Donny Ouyang, founded website development and marketing company Kinksaro Tech Limited at age 13

Automate Your Giving

If you know you want to give the American Red Cross $120 every year for disaster relief, set up a savings account for your business. (Look for one that doesn't have a minimum balance or fees.) Then set up a monthly $10 automatic transfer from your company checking account into your disaster relief account. Voilà! At the end of the year, the money will be there waiting for you to put it to good use.

Treat Your Vendors Right

You know you need to treat your customers right; that's just part of good customer service, as was talked about in Chapter 8. But it's also important to be ethical in your dealings with the people who supply the materials you need to operate. If you have a good vendor, stay loyal. Sometimes other vendors will attempt to bribe you to use their product or service, but that's not cool. Not only are you leaving the vendor who's been good to you, but accepting gifts from vendors is unethical and even illegal in some industries. Many executives and government employees have gotten into big trouble for doing this. So if you buy doggie treats for your pet-walking service from a wholesaler on the east side, but the wholesaler on the west side offers you concert tickets if you switch to him, resist temptation and walk the other way. And treat your vendors well; paying all invoices on time and in full helps keep another business running, and you know how important that is.

Be a Philanthropist

One of the most common ways businesses give back is through philanthropy, which involves using your resources to benefit others. As an entrepreneur, one of the most obvious resources you possess is money—but it's probably a good idea to wait until you're turning an actual profit to start passing out cash! Still, every philanthropist has to start somewhere, and getting in the giving habit now will prepare you to be an even bigger giver later. The key to making maximum impact no matter how much money you have to spare is to align your business with a cause that really matters to you. That way it won't feel like torture to donate. So if you're all about the environment, think about giving to Greenpeace. Or if finding a cure for cancer is important to you, contact the Breast Cancer Research Foundation. Philanthropy can also mean donating time and resources, like building a website for a local charity of your choice. However you decide to give back, build it into your business model. It's cool to decide one day that you want to drop a few bucks on a charity, but putting it in your business plan will help you be more consistent with your giving and ensure that you actually have the resources to make it happen when the time comes.

There are three main ways you can leverage your business to do good when it comes to philanthropy.

* **Donate.** You can make a monetary donation every month or at the end of each year; even just $100 annually can make a significant impact for a cause. Or you can donate your actual product or service. For example, if you run an interior design company, you can spruce up the shelter downtown. Design websites? You could create or update one for a local nonprofit to help it better serve its beneficiaries.

* **Work for charity.** You can use your company to do actual work for a nonprofit. So if you run a moving company, you could use your trucks to collect donations for the annual coat drive in your town. Or you could ask your team of party DJs to spin at one charity event a month.

* **Provide strategic discounts.** You can directly benefit members of your community by offering discounts to disadvantaged customers. So if you have a house painting business, you could offer reduced prices for families in low-income neighborhoods. If snow removal is your thing, you could dig out the driveways of your elderly neighbors for half your usual fee.

* **Be a lender.** You know that it takes money to start a business, so give a loan to someone who needs one. Microfinance services combine your funds with money from tons of other private lenders, so even a very small loan will go to use.

Take a few minutes to brainstorm ways that you can flex your philanthropic muscles.

> *I think philanthropy should be an ongoing thing. If I were a billionaire, I wouldn't do anything but help people solve their problems. I know that sounds kinda cheesy, but I just really like to help people! I see how a lot of people helped me with my life. I have a personal goal to donate $1 million by the time I'm 22. Philanthropy is part of my business model, too; we've given to the Hurricane Katrina fund and the Salvation Army, and we've always done free stuff for people, especially seniors.*
>
> —Blaine Mickens, founded landscaping company Estate Groomers at age 14

Be a Mentor

Philanthropy isn't the only way you can use your business to do good. You can also help people who want to be entrepreneurs just like you. Chapter 2 discussed mentors, those people who are currently showing you the way as you develop your company. But that street runs both ways. You can also be a mentor to another aspiring entrepreneur. "But I don't know anything yet!" you might protest. Not true. When you first had an inkling of an idea to start a company, you might have known nothing, but now you've written a business plan, trademarked your company's name, financed your operations, and maybe

even hired a staff. You're doing big things! You could teach a kid who is getting started *a ton* about how to do it right. It's truly a process; even the biggest entrepreneurs you can name still consult with their mentors, even as they start helping other people come up. Richard Branson—the billionaire who founded Virgin Records, Virgin Airlines, the environmentally conscious Virgin Green Fund, and the nonprofit social entrepreneurial foundation Virgin Unite—has several mentors whom he talks to regularly, including human rights activist Archbishop Desmond Tutu, former Secretary-General of the United Nations Kofi Annan, and reknowned environmentalist and scientist James Lovelock. It's never too early to be a mentor. Whether you advise one person until you're both old and gray or take on one new person every year, it feels wonderful to get someone else started on the path to independence. Plus, you get to sharpen your own skills as you go. It's a win-win situation.

There are a few different ways to take on the responsibility of being a mentor. Which method you choose will depend on the amount of time and level of interest you have. Just be sure you commit fully: If you promise to meet with someone each month, it's your duty to do it. You'd be upset if *your* mentor were a flake, so it's important that you hold yourself to the same standard. Here are some ways to find someone to mentor.

✸ **Take on an intern.** An intern is someone who works for you for little or no money or even for school credit in exchange for learning how to do what you do. Generally, interns want to work in the same field you do. So if you repair computers, you'd hire someone who wants to do that one day. Interns are pretty easy to find. The computer kid might belong to the tech club down at the middle

I started hosting entrepreneur workshops for young kids during my sophomore year in high school. I did it because, when I was starting my company, a lot of kids made comments like, "I didn't know you could start a business that young" and "Is that even possible?" There was a real lack of knowledge. But now kids are learning about independence, success, goals, and financial stability. They will be our future business minds.

—Gabrielle McBay, founded cookie company Crumbs by Gabrielle at age 13

school, so you could ask the teacher who runs it to recommend someone or ask to speak to the entire club one day and talk to anyone who's interested. Just be sure to follow the government's internship guidelines (see the Resources section at the end of the chapter for more info), and let your intern do more than grunt work. Sure she can go to customers' homes to pick up broken hardware, but she should get some time to sit next to you while you run diagnostics programs and fix the problem. It's the only way for her to learn.

✸ **Join a local program.** You can also find someone through local entrepreneur programs. You might have already joined Junior Achievement to find your own mentor. Ask about pairing with a newcomer to provide advice as he gets his company started. It's not important that you be in the same industry, either. As you know, there are certain skills that you need to develop no matter what kind of business you have, so your experience in running a personal

coaching company will definitely benefit someone who wants to start installing car sound systems.

✸ **Search the internet.** You don't actually have to see the person you mentor in real life. There are entire websites developed to virtually connecting mentors and students, whether you eventually meet in person or keep your relationship digital. Mentori.org matches you with people in developing countries, and MicroMentor.org offers opportunities to mentor on specific topics, such as marketing your service effectively or building a hot website.

Take a few minutes to brainstorm how you can help other aspiring entrepreneurs to get started. 🖥

Go Green

Part of doing good is caring not only about how your business affects people but how it affects the planet. It's up to all of us to do our part—both in our personal lives and at work—to protect the environment.

Quiz! How Green Are You?

Think you're an environmental expert? Take our quiz to see just how on it you are, then learn ways to use what you know to green your business—and the world.

1. **When the grocery store cashier asks "paper or plastic?" you say:**
   a. "Paper."
   b. "Plastic."
   c. "Neither—I brought my own!"

2. **At the end of the day, you:**
   a. Turn off your laptop.
   b. Unplug your energy-efficient netbook. Computers are serious power vampires, even when they're off.
   c. Leave your desktop computer running—it makes it easier to check your email before class in the morning.

3. **Your fave piece of clothing is made out of:**
   a. Bamboo.
   b. Leather.
   c. Organic cotton.

4. **You think "fair trade":**
   a. Is when you give your older sister a CD and she gives you the car keys for the afternoon.
   b. Has something to do with the rainforest, right?
   c. Is awesome because it pays farmers better wages and encourages sustainable growing and harvesting practices.

5. **You're headed to the gym to break a sweat. You:**
   a. Grab a plastic bottle of water on the way out the door.
   b. Fill up your no-BPA aluminum bottle with filtered water.
   c. Drink from the water fountain between sets.

6. **You think "TRNF LTS" means:**
   a. Transfer letters?
   b. Turn off the lights, of course.
   c. Sorry, I don't speak crazy person.

7. The thing you love most about your generation is that:

a. You're all about saving energy.

b. You have so many cool electronic gadgets.

c. Hold that thought—you need to go charge your mp3 player.

8. It's time to deliver copies of your latest zine issue. You:

a. Pack the day with errands so you can handle all your business in one car trip.

b. Gas up your mom's SUV.

c. Throw them in your bike's basket and get pedaling.

9. A community garden sounds like a place:

a. To spend a relaxing Sunday afternoon.

b. Your mom or dad should visit before making dinner.

c. For old people to congregate.

10. In the summer you like to:

a. Head outdoors to your favorite shady spot and chill.

b. Use your ceiling fan to stay comfortable.

c. Crank up the AC as far as it can go.

KEY			
1.	a: 2	b: 3	c: 1
2.	a: 2	b: 1	c: 3
3.	a: 1	b: 3	c: 2
4.	a: 3	b: 2	c: 1
5.	a: 3	b: 1	c: 2
6.	a: 2	b: 1	c: 3
7.	a: 1	b: 2	c: 3
8.	a: 2	b: 3	c: 1
9.	a: 3	b: 2	c: 1
10.	a: 1	b: 2	c: 3

24 to 30 Points: Mint Green

So you probably don't *hate* the earth, but you don't really think about it much either. Is there something wrong with that? Well, yes, actually. The thing is, as an entrepreneur, you have a greater responsibility than your typical teenager. Why? Because you have *influence*. Whether it's your employees or your clients, people are watching what you do and taking notes. Luckily, it's easy to paint yourself a darker shade of green—just take baby steps. Start by reading a few blogs on the topic so you can learn more, then follow the tips later in this chapter. Every day, little by little, you'll inch closer to a green life and a green business.

17 to 23 Points: Kelly Green

You *kinda* know what you should be doing, but you aren't always willing to do it—especially if it feels like an inconvenience. So your first step toward being more eco-friendly is to try to make it as easy as possible. There are tons of super simple tips later in this chapter. Once you get the ball rolling, you can think of specific ways to make your business greener. Make taking care of the environment a natural part of your business operations, and it'll be easier to keep it up.

10 to 16 Points: Forest Green

Talk about hard core: You know that every little thing counts, you're always up on all the latest green news, and you're never too busy to be Mother Nature's BFF. Plus you know that what you do influences others, so you strive to set a good example at all times. You're already doing all that you can on a personal level. Make an even bigger difference by applying the stuff you do in your everyday life to how you run your company. The Earth will thank you.

Green Your Business

No matter how green you are now, there's always more to be done. Running a business that's sustainable (which means that it meets the company's needs but won't harm the planet for future generations) is easy if you establish good environmental practices from the get-go. Here are some ways to do that:

☀ **Don't waste paper.** Do as much billing as you can via the web so you can limit your use of physical paper. When you must print stuff, buy recycled paper and use both sides.

☀ **Paper or plastic? Neither.** Skip disposable plastic bags and containers in favor of reusable ones.

☀ **Power down.** Turn lights, computers, and other work-based electrical equipment off every night. To help remember to do this, put all of it—your laptop, printer, desk lamp, pencil sharpener—on an energy-saving "smart" power strip. When you turn off your computer each night, the power to everything else will also turn off.

☀ **Shine on.** Buy energy-saving compact fluorescent light bulbs for the lamp on your desk or, better yet, an LED bulb.

☀ **Unplug!** Though you may need to charge your cell phone over night, unplug the charger when you grab your phone in the morning since the charger still drains juice even when your phone is not charging. Same goes for all chargers.

☀ **Greenify.** Buy a plant or two to clean the air in your workspace and reduce indoor pollution.

☀ **Conserve fuel.** When you have a ton of deliveries to make, plan your route to use the least amount of gas—or better yet, ride your bike.

You can even carry your eco-friendly attitude into your specific business practices. For example, if you repair laptops, use energy-efficient hard drives to replace the corrupted ones (then recycle the old parts—the manufacturer can tell you how). Or if you paint bedrooms, use low-VOC paint to reduce indoor air pollution for your clients. If you organize video game tournaments, borrow your mom's glasses for drinks instead of using disposable plastic cups. Or buy aluminum water bottles for your

> *We're an online publishing platform and consulting group, so we're pretty green by the nature of our business. While our primary focus is youth empowerment, we designed the website in ways aimed at reducing energy usage from readers' computers, and we work to raise awareness and funds for several environmental nonprofits.*
>
> —Crystal Yan, founded book project What's Next: 25 Big Ideas from Gen-Yers Under 25 *at age 17*

moving crew so they can rehydrate responsibly on every job and not have to waste all those plastic bottles. If you deliver food to the masses, use biodegradable products to reduce your contribution to the local landfill. And when you change the oil for your car repair clients, use synthetic oil instead of the petroleum-based stuff. In many cases you'll save money. For example, shutting off electronics can save big bucks on the electric bill. And you may also gain clients. If you promote your company's green practices whenever you can by listing them on your website and in other marketing materials, you'll create goodwill for your company. All things being equal, many people will go with a green business over its competitors. Brainstorm ways that you can make your business more environmentally friendly.

Your Company's Commandments

One way to be sure your company is an ethical one is to develop a set of commandments, or rules, that you operate by. That way, if you're ever in doubt as to what to do in a particular situation, you and your employees can refer back to your rules for guidance. You could have a commandment about always paying people a good wage, donating five percent of your profits to charity each year, or never using overblown claims in your advertising. It's really up to you. Just be sure your commandments touch on how you'll handle your employees, your vendors, the environment, and, last but not least, your customers. Write your own

Ten Ethics Commandments. Your advisors could also be a huge help on this one.

Resources

GuideStar.org
This site helps you find charities that match your interests and even lets you check to see how they will spend your donation.

Youth.Foundationcenter.org
Use this organization to connect with other teens who care and to find tools for giving. (Note that this site address doesn't contain "www" like the rest do.)

Kiva.org
You can use this microfinancing site to loan money to budding entrepreneurs in developing nations.

DOL.gov
Search "Fact sheet #71" on the United States Department of Labor's website for internship guidelines *before* you find an intern.

Mentori.org
This site matches you with people in developing countries who need business guidance.

MicroMentor.org
Here you can provide expert advice on your business specialty, whether it's building great websites from scratch or creating buzz with social networking.

Earth911.com
This is the place to go for great tips on greening your business, including how to recycle *everything*, from car batteries to latex paint.

Treehugger.com
This site is all about making sustainable living—and working— fun and easy.

CHAPTER 10

NOW WHAT?

To Grow or Let It Go

At some point, every entrepreneur is faced with a tough question: "Now what should I do with my business?" It's no different for a teen tycoon. If the business is doing well, you might think about expanding and going national. If you're getting bored, maybe you want to sell it and start another. You also need to consider what to do with the business when high school is over. Do you take it with you when it's time to go to college? Move on completely and focus on your education? And what if it gets to be too big? Do you bring in more people or let other things go so that you can work on it more hours each week? You're already making so many decisions at this time that the idea of one more might seem as appealing as coming clean to your crush in front of the entire school. But your company is your baby, and you need to think carefully about what you do with it as your life situation changes.

What Was Your Goal Again?

Earlier in the book, you figured out your goals for your business. When it comes time to consider your next move, the first step is to revisit those objectives.

Start with your financial goals. If you've already achieved them (for instance, you've bought that car or made enough money to pay for your first year of college), perhaps you won't see any need to continue running your company. Or maybe you want to continue it in some way but not necessarily expand it. Or maybe revisiting your goals will show that you are now ready to aim higher, and hiring a slew of employees can take your company to the next level.

Now reevaluate your personal goals. Perhaps you don't just want to be the leading babysitting company in your town but you want to take over the whole state. Or maybe you started your babysitting business to get experience in dealing with kids and now you want to focus on going to school for a degree in education so you can teach third grade. Whatever your goals, they will affect your next step. When you've figured out your updated personal and financial goals, write them in your notebook.

> When it was time to go to college, I thought to myself, "We have these customers who like what we're doing and we've got these tutors who enjoy working for us, so we have to keep this going." It was that simple. If it's something you're really passionate about, you make the time for it, and I think there's plenty of time in college to run something. So I got a Blackberry in 2004—it was huge!—and I set up my class schedule so that I could work.
>
> —Erik Kimel, founded tutoring company Peer2Peer Tutors, LLC at age 17

Next Moves Flowchart

Now that you've reconsidered your goals, it's time to decide what to do with your company. Pick the brains of your trusty mentors or advisors, then use this flowchart to help you figure out how to move forward with your business.

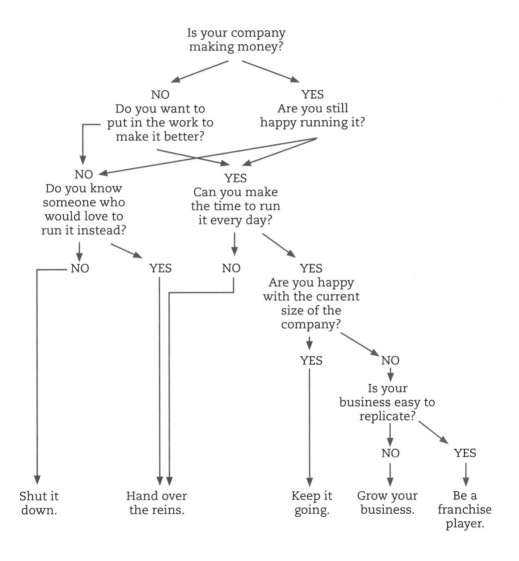

Keeping It Going

You're in the sweet spot: Your company is working perfectly for you! Why take on the extra headaches of expanding it if you're having fun *and* making all the money you need and want already? (And if you're heading to college right now, you're already adding a lot to your plate.) Just keep referring back to your business plan to be sure you're on the right track and don't be afraid to make changes in the name of flexibility. Enjoy!

Pros: You are still doing what makes you happy in the way that makes you happy.

Cons: Your earnings might not increase over time.

Growing Your Business

Taking your business to the next level is exciting! Whether you just want to make some more cash each month or you're moving to a new place for college and want to keep things going, there are plenty of opportunities for growth. The key to successful expansion is to do it at the right time. For most entrepreneurs, that time comes when you find that you are spending more time managing the business than you're spending actually doing the work of the business. For example, if you run a photography business and you're too busy handling the schedule to go out and take pictures, it's probably time to hire some help! Or maybe the time will come when you look up and realize that your company has the potential to be much larger. Just listen to your heart—and your business' bank account—and move accordingly.

The first step in expanding your company is to sit down and figure out how you can make it work. There are three main ways to grow your business. They often overlap, so moving to the next level will likely require some combination of them.

✸ **Hire employees.** If you're mowing half the lawns in your neighborhood alone and you don't have enough time to handle the other half, it might make sense to hire a friend or sibling to help you. That way, you can please more clients and make even more money.

✸ **Add a new service or product.** If you have all the mowing needs of your neighborhood on lock, maybe you can increase your profits by adding hedge trimming and leaf raking to your repertoire. Or keep things going in the winter by adding a snow shoveling service.

✿ **Market to a new audience.** If you're already handling all the lawns in your neighborhood, you could start offering your expertise to the next town over. Or if you've been focusing on residential lawns (the grass outside private homes), you could add commercial clients and mow the grounds outside office buildings and malls. Moving to a new town for school can provide an easy way to expand; you could open a branch of your lawn care company in your new town and hire someone to run the day-to-day operations in your hometown. Just like that, you've doubled the size of your company! But of course, this only works if there is a need for your product or service in your new spot; you might not get any grass-cutting love if there's already an established business there. So do your research first, survey your competitors and potential customers, and see where your company fits into the mix. Perhaps you can beat the local favorite on price or superior customer service.

Once you decide which expansion methods to use, take your time. Remember that picture book about the tortoise and the hare? The moral of the story was that slow and steady wins the race. That should be your mantra as you expand. So many entrepreneurs don't act like that wise tortoise, and they end up in a bad place. Here's an example: You have been successful selling handmade jewelry at local events, so you decide to sell your pieces online.

The Tip Jar TIPS

Ask for Help

Some of what makes growing your business daunting is the fear of putting even more work on your plate since you're already crazy busy! But delegating tasks will save you a ton of time and worry. So if you have to add online sales to your site, pay someone else to do it rather than add it to your to-do list. And when the time comes to expand your house-painting business to homes across town, ask your cousin who lives there to give you a hand. You'll save a bunch of time in the long run, and that's really your most valuable resource.

> *My business has expanded over the past year by gaining customers from all over. My first contract with OmniPeace stated that my licensed territory was the United States. Soon my territory expanded to the world!*
>
> —Alexa Carlin, founded OmniPeace jewelry line Alexa Rose at age 17

And you get a huge rush of holiday orders! Unfortunately, there's no way you can make 1,913 pieces *and* study for finals, so you end up fulfilling only half of the orders in time. The result: Customers get upset and post negative reviews on your website, and your business drops off. Sucks, right?

Don't be *that* entrepreneur. Take a breath and make sure you are prepared to take on the extra work that comes with expansion. In this scenario, you could have avoided the bad feedback if you had hired some friends to help fulfill the online orders. Yeah, it would have cost you a few bucks, but you would have had a bunch of new, satisfied customers. Once you have a realistic, workable plan for expansion, start making things happen, whether it means renting kitchen space to bake your cookies or hiring a consultant to install audio systems back home.

Pros: Your company will grow, and you'll still be doing what you love.

Cons: A larger company means more demands on your time.

Be a Franchise Player

If you have a business that is easy to replicate, you might want to try creating a franchise. That's when you sell the rights to use your company assets (think: name, logo, business model) to other would-be business owners. It's how Subway and Ace Hardware are constantly opening new locations. Doing this changes the way you run your business, though. Instead of selling your product or service, you will in essence be selling your business. And you'll have to be extremely vigilant that franchises uphold your level of service; a customer shouldn't be able to see any difference among locations.

Opting to franchise is a big decision, and you need to ask yourself some hard questions: Is your business really amazing? Do you have a super unique concept that others would be interested in implementing in their neighborhoods? Would you feel bad about having other people run parts of your business? If your answers are "yes," "yes," and "no," this might be the right path for you. Do a ton of research into the subject and get a lawyer to help you price your franchises and do the (extensive) paperwork. Welcome to the big leagues.

Pros: Your business gets to be in two—or more—places at once, and you have a new way of making money.

Cons: Your company could get really large, really quickly, making it easy to lose track of what's going on, especially if you're simultaneously making your way through college life. Also, you'll be paying your lawyer plenty for her help.

Shut It Down

That old saying about how "All good things must come to an end" isn't necessarily true, but there is something to be said for knowing when to move on. If you need to spend more time on your schoolwork, dread getting out of bed early on the weekends to run your business, or find that it's still costing you more money than it's making you (after sticking with it for a while, of course), it might be time to move on to your next dream. Why do something that doesn't make you happy?

If you decide to move on, there's a way it should be done—and a way it *shouldn't* be done. It might be tempting to just close up shop, but it's good practice to notify folks properly. Apart from the fact that it's just the right thing to do, it will leave you with a solid reputation should you decide to start another business down the line.

Update your website to show that you've gone out of business, and if you're running any advertisements (online or anywhere else), now's the time to pull them. If you have regular customers, alert them that you're shutting down the company and refer them to another service if you know of one. And if people

How I Started My Business

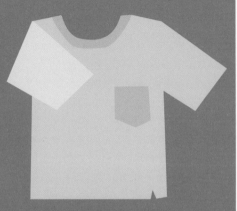

I entered a T-shirt design contest and decided to draw pictures of African-American inventions on my T-shirt. I won, and it made me realize that a lot of clothes my peers thought were really cool didn't have much significance behind them. I thought it'd be cool to create my own shirts to wear to show my friends the contributions of African-Americans— I wanted to have some sort of purpose and educate others about something that's often left out of American history classes. All my friends wanted to buy my clothes, and then their parents wanted to order shirts from me. That's what encouraged me to keep going.

— Tevyn Cole, founded clothing design company School Me at age 10

lent you money, remember that you still need to pay them back. If you don't have the money to do this, work out a payment plan with them immediately. If someone invested in your company, let them know you're ready to pull out. Refer to your original agreement to see if you owe them anything at this stage. And remember: You still need to file your taxes for your final year; check out the "Closing a Business Checklist" on the IRS website for tips on how to make a clean break from your company (see the Resources section at the end of this chapter).

Pros: You can focus your energy on things that are more important to you.

Cons: You will lose the independence and income that comes from running your own business—unless you start another.

Hand Over the Reins

Just because you don't want to run the business anymore doesn't mean that it's not a dream gig for someone else. It doesn't mean that you have to leave the company completely, either. Do you have an employee who would jump at the chance to run the company, while you take a smaller role that better fits into your schedule? Or maybe your partner can manage it during the school year and you can manage it during the summer? Alternately, you could give it up completely—if your little sister has been helping you put together furniture, maybe she'd like to keep things going when you leave. Just make sure that the person who takes over will maintain your high standards of service. You don't want your company name tarnished, especially if you're still working behind the scenes.

Below are some steps you need to take to sell your company. (If you're just taking a step back, it might not be necessary to complete all these steps, especially if you plan to run things again down the road; discuss it with the new CEO.) Don't

hesitate to ask your mentor and advisors for help anytime you need it.

✸ **Consider hiring a lawyer.** Selling your company can be as easy as asking a buyer for five times as much money as you took in last year or as complicated as hiring an appraiser to go through your books, haggling over a price, and revising a contract a million times. If things get crazy, you'll be glad to have someone by your side who has been there before.

✸ **Identify the person who wants to take over for you.** It makes sense to ask around inside your company first. The people who work with you know the most about the company and are in the best position to make a seamless transition. If no one there is interested but you really want to sell it and move on, search entrepreneurship websites for aspiring business owners in your industry and ask your mentor to help you find someone.

✸ **Interview all interested parties.** You want to make sure that the person who takes over is really committed to the vision. You'll kick yourself if the next owner runs your business into the ground. Just like when you hired people

> *I put my business on hold completely for my freshman and sophomore years of college, but I wish I hadn't done this. I knew I might want to pick it back up eventually, and I shouldn't have dropped it. I finally picked it back up again junior year, but getting it restarted was really hard. If you know you want to keep your business alive, make sure you put in a few hours a week to keep it going.*
>
> *—Vanessa Van Patten, founded teen-run parenting advice company Radical Parenting at age 16*

way back when, pick the person who will do the best job, not the person you like best.

* **Agree on terms.** Do you want the new person to take over as CEO, while you handle deliveries? Do you want to step away completely? You need to figure this out before you sign anything, especially if you plan to continue working for the company in a different capacity.

* **Negotiate a fair price for your company.** The price should cover any equipment that you're passing on, keep you rolling in cash at least until you get a job or start a new business, and take into consideration the start-up funds you sank in the beginning, outstanding loans, and the potential earnings the business could net the

new owner. Your mentor can be a huge help in determining how much you can make for your company.

* **Sign a contract.** The Small Business Administration can help you with writing a contract (see the Resources section for more info), but do make sure it includes a list of everything you're selling (from the actual business to any supplies and tools), the price, how and when you will receive the money, how and when business information will be handed over, what role you will continue to have in the company (if any), and the date when the company will officially change ownership. Even if you decided to complete the sale without a lawyer, have one take a look at this agreement before you both sign.

* **Transfer ownership if you're backing out completely.** This includes the transfer of any outstanding loans. The "Sale of a Business" page on the IRS website and the Small Business Administration can guide you through the process (see Resources).

* **Pass on records and contacts.** From customer order records to the phone number for the guy who keeps you flush with wholesale cleaning supplies for your maid service, now's the time to hand them over. The new owner will need them to maintain the business. Also remember to transfer control of the website so it can be updated without your help.

Pros: Your customers will still have their needs met, and you can make some money on the sale.

Cons: You might have a difficult time seeing someone else running your baby, even if you are ready to move on.

Resources

IRS.gov/businesses
This site is a huge help if you decide to shutter or sell your business. Just click on "Closing a Business" and then the "Closing a Business Checklist" to see what you need to do to close it, or "Sale of a Business" for help with your sale.

SBA.gov/smallbusinessplanner
This is a great resource for advice on how to sell your business, including what should be in a seller's agreement and how to decide how much you should get for it.

Franchise.org
Go here for a walk through the steps for franchising your business, courtesy of the International Franchise Association.

Index

A

Abraham, Jack, 80, 86, 90, 97
Abramson, Josh, 13
AccionUSA.org, 81
accountants, 63
Ace Hardware, 144
adult perspectives, 15–16, 101, 104, 117. *See also* family
advertising. *See* marketing
advisors, 30, 55, 109, 120. *See also* mentors
age barriers, 10, 16, 117
agreements, 73, 148
Alexa Rose, 17, 35, 68, 144
Alexander, Amiya, 15, 50
Amiya's Mobile Dance Academy, 15, 50
Annan, Kofi, 129
Apple computers, 100
Aronica, Lou, 24
audience. *See also* customers; marketing
    expanding, 143
    identifying target, 100
    reaching, 103
    sales (elevator) pitch to, 108–109

B

banking, 16, 70, 71, 72, 75
BankRate.com, 63
Barlow, Janelle, 121
Ben & Jerry's, 33
Benfari, Robert, 97
Berger, Jeff, 25, 84, 103
Bing.com, 111
Blogger.com, 111

blogging, 106, 111
board of advisors, 30, 120
book authorship, 12, 20, 37
boss. *See* management
brainstorming
    audience target, 100
    board of advisors, 30
    business niche, 24
    competitive edge, 100
    eco-friendly practices, 136
    financial goals, 74–75
    goals and purpose, 13
    marketing avenues, 103, 105
    mentorship, giving back, 131
    names of business, 54–56
    passion, 16, 24
    as routine process, 88–89
    staff positions needed, 84–85
brand building, 121, 124, 125
Branson, Richard, 129–130
Bridgeforth, David, 29, 60, 124
Brown, Les, 60
budget worksheet, 46
budgeting, 46, 65. *See also* money
business ownership. *See also* entrepreneurs
    franchise, 144–145, 149
    obstacles to, 15–16
    partnering vs. sole, 30–35
    rewards of, 14–15
    transferring, 149
    types/niches of, 16, 18–24

business plan
    about, 39–41
    resources, 51
    sample, 42–49
Business.gov, 58, 61, 63, 81

C

capital. *See also* costs
    asking for, 72–74, 78
    needs, estimating, 66–68
    sources of, 70–71
card design, greeting, 20, 30, 33, 125
cards, business, 104
Carlin, Alexa, 17, 35, 66, 144
cell phone apps, 19, 75
charity. *See* giving back
Cohen, Ben, 33
Cole, Tevyn, 88, 109, 146
college transition, 139, 140
CollegeHumor.com, 13
Colombo, George, 121
commandments, 136–137
communication. *See also* feedback
    coaching, 29, 60
    customer service best practices, 116–117
    as entrepreneurial trait, 11–12
    with mentors, 28
    polite (etiquette), 116, 117–118
    shutting down, 145–146
    speaking, 108–109, 117
community. *See* giving back; social networks

company. *See also* business
   ownership
   commandments of,
      136–137
   expanding, 142–145
   franchising, 144–145, 149
   legal structure of, 58–59
   licensing and registration,
      61
   location of, 15, 67, 144–145
   names, 54–58, 57, 58, 61, 63
   restarting, 148
   selling your, 147–149
   setup resources, 63
   shutting down, 145–147
   tax setup of, 61–63
   trademarking, 56, 57, 63
competition
   comparing, 76–77
   edge on, 100
   partnering with, 103
A Complaint Is a Gift (Barlow
   and Moller), 121
complaints, customer, 114,
   115
contractors, 84, 90
contracts, 73, 148, 174
corporate structure, 59
costs. *See also* payments
   earning money vs., 75–76
   location, 67
   operating, 66–68
   payroll, 89–90
   pricing and, 75–78
   start-up, 44, 66
   trademarking, 56

Crumbs by Gabrielle, 10, 116,
   130
customer service. *See also*
   feedback
   benefits of, 115
   best practices, top five, 114,
      116–117
   etiquette, 116, 117–118
   internet resources for, 121
customers. *See also* marketing
   bad, letting go of, 120
   complaints from, 114, 115,
      120
   loyalty building, 121
   market analysis, 100–102
   reviews from, 114
   surveying, 55, 101–102, 111,
      119, 121
   thanking, 116

D
DeCotiis, Tom, 121
delegation, 143, 144
design
   card, 20, 30, 33, 125
   clothing, 4–5, 20, 110, 146
   graphic, 20
   interior, 20
   website development, 22,
      40, 89, 111
discounts, 128
domain names, 58
donations, 127, 128. *See also*
   gifts; giving back

E
earning money, 74–76
Earth911.com, 137
eco-friendly practices, 131–
   136, 137
EINs. *See* Employer
   Identification Numbers
*The Element: How Finding
   Your Passion Changes
   Everything* (Robinsonn
   and Aronica), 24
elevator pitch, 108–109
email, 28, 105, 118
employees. *See* staff
Employer Identification
   Numbers (EINs), 61–62
Entrepreneur.com, 24, 51, 97
entrepreneurs
   development resources, 24,
      28, 29, 36
   goals and purpose for, 13
   responsibility of, 130, 134
   traits of, 10–13
   types of, 20–24
environment. *See* eco-friendly
   practices; work
   environment
Estate Groomers, 34, 57, 74,
   120, 129
ethical treatment
   commandments for,
      136–137
   of environment, 135–136
   of staff, 126
   of vendors, 127
etiquette, 116, 117–118

Etsy.com, 106, 111
events, marketing via, 109
expansion, 142–145
expenses. *See* costs

F
Facebook, 104, 105, 107. *See also* social networks
family, 15–16, 33, 35, 86–88
feedback. *See also* advisors; mentors
    bad, 101, 114, 115, 120
    changes based on, 120
    customer reviews, 114
    incentives for, 119
    open to, being, 29
    opportunities for, 118–119
    surveys for, 55, 101–102, 111, 119, 121
finances. *See also* costs; income
    accountants, 63
    break-even point, 72
    budget worksheet, 46
    on business plan sample, 44–46
    charity as benefit to, 124
    goals for, 74–75, 140
    investors, 45, 71, 72
    tracking, 75, 79–80
flyers, 104
Franchise.org, 149
franchising, 144–145, 149
Free Mania, 41, 69, 78
friends, 30, 86–88
funding. *See* capital

G
gifts, as capital source, 71
giving back. *See also* ethical treatment
    automating, 127

benefits of, 124–126
in business plan sample, 48–49
commandments for, 136–137
to the environment, 135–136, 137
Helper types, 21
    as mentor, 129–131
    philanthropic, 127–128
    stories of, 17
goals. *See also* vision
    commandments and, 136–137
    financial, 74–75, 140
    purpose and, 13
    revisiting, 140
    setting, as entrepreneurial trait, 11
Godin, Seth, 37
Google search results, 106, 108
Gorog, Chris, 4–5
government filings, 56, 61–63
grants, 71, 81
green business. *See* eco-friendly practices
Greenfield, Jerry, 33
GuideStar.org, 137

H
handbills, 104
Harlem Lyrics, 30, 33, 101, 125
HeadlineShirts.com, 4–5
help, asking for, 12, 15–16, 27, 28, 143. *See also* feedback
hiring, 25, 85–86, 142, 147–148
Holloman, Chauncey, 30, 33, 101, 125
human resources. *See* staff

I
income. *See also* capital; finances
    earning money, 74–77
    pricing and, 75–78
    reinvesting, 78–79
Indinero.com, 79, 81
insurance, 67–68
Internal Revenue Service, 62, 63, 146, 149
internet resources. *See also* social networks
    business plan, 51
    company setup, 63
    customer service, 121
    eco-friendly business, 131, 137
    entrepreneur development, 24, 28, 29, 36
    legal structure setup, 58, 63
    marketing, 105–108, 111
    mentors, 28, 36, 131, 137
    money management, 81
    staff management, 97
internet start-ups, 4–5, 13, 25, 69, 80, 89
interns, 130–131
Intuit.com, 105, 111
investors, 45, 71, 72
IRS. *See* Internal Revenue Service

J
Junior Achievement, 28, 36, 131

K
karma, 124–125
Killer Customer Care (Colombo), 121

Kimel, Erik, 107, 115, 140Kinksaro Tech Limited, 40, 89, 126
Kiva.org, 128, 137
Kiyosaki, Robert T., 81
KODA, 25, 84, 103

L
lawyers, 147
leadership, 13
Lechter, Sharon L., 81
legal structure, 58–59. *See also* government filings
LegalZoom.com, 58, 63
licenses, 61
limited liability company (LLC), 59
loans, 71, 72, 73, 81, 128, 137
location management, 15, 67, 144–145
losses, taking, 120, 145–146
Lovelock, James, 130
loyalty, 121, 127

M
mailers, 104
Make It Glow (DeCotiis), 121
management team. *See also* staff
    building, 30, 42–43, 120, 147–148
    styles, 92–96
market analysis, 100–102
marketing
    avenues for, 103–108
    in business plan sample, 47–48
    efficient multitasking, 105
    as entrepreneurial trait, 12–13
    events and parties for, 109
    expanding, 143

free, SEO for, 106
internet, 105–108, 111
low-tech, 104–105
through partnerships, 103
sales (elevator) pitch for, 108–109
McBay, Gabrielle, 10, 116, 130
meetings, 29, 118
Meetup.com, 29, 36
Mentori.org, 131, 137
mentors
    finding, 28–29, 36, 131, 137
    giving back as, 129–131
    internet resources, 28, 36, 131, 137
    interns and, 130–131
    parents as, 35
Mickens, Blaine, 34, 57, 74, 120, 129
microfinancing, 81, 128, 137
micromanaging, 96
MicroMentor.org, 131, 137
Milo.com, 80, 86, 90, 97
Moller, Claus, 121
money. *See also* capital; costs; finances; income
    asking for, 72–74
    earning, 74–77
    management, 11, 81
    partnership choice for, 30–31
    reinvesting, 78–79
    from savings, 16, 70
multitasking, 12, 105
My Biggest Mistake... And How I Fixed It (Pledger), 97

N
names
    company, 54–58, 57, 58, 61, 63

customer, best practices and, 116
Network for Teaching Entrepreneurship (NFTE), 81
networking, 107, 109. *See also* social networks
niche, finding, 16, 18–24
note-taking, 10, 13. *See also* brainstorming

O
office. *See* location management; work environment
OmniPeace, 17, 35, 68, 144
online communities. *See* social networks
operating costs, 66–68
opinions. *See* feedback
organization. *See* planning; record keeping
Ouyang, Danny, 40, 89, 126
overhead, estimating, 67
ownership. *See* business ownership; entrepreneurs

P
paperwork, 62. *See also* record keeping
parents, 15–16, 33, 35, 67, 86–88
partnership. *See also* sole proprietorship
    capital raising from, 70
    choosing, 30–31
    for promotion, 103
    pros and cons of, 33, 35
passion, 11, 16, 24. *See also* vision
paychecks. *See* wages

payments
    to self, 76
    to staff, 89–90, 126
    to vendors, 127, 146
Peer2Peer Tutors, LLC, 107,
    115, 140
people management. *See* staff
people-persons, 21
permits, 61
philanthropy, 127–128. *See
    also* giving back
phone conversations, 117
pitch, sales (elevator), 108–109
planning. *See also* business
    plan
    as entrepreneurial trait, 11
    giving back automation,
        127
    Helper-type niche and, 21
    for meetings, 29
    party, 21
    priority lists for, 31
Pledger, Marcia, 97
politeness. *See* etiquette
press releases, 109–110
pricing, 75–78
prioritization, 31
profit, 16, 65, 72, 78. *See also*
    income
promoting. *See* marketing
purchases. *See* transactions
purpose. *See* goals; passion

Q
quizzes, 18–24, 92–96, 132–134
    eco-friendly business,
        132–134
    management/boss types,
        92–96
    niche finding, 18–24

R
Radical Parenting, 55, 91, 106,
    148
Rankin, Kenrya, 4, 156
record keeping, 22, 62, 75,
    79–80, 117, 149
recruitment, 25, 85–86. *See
    also* hiring
repeat business, 113, 115. *See
    also* customer service
resources. *See* internet
    resources
revenue models, 74–77
revenue services, state, 62–63
reviews, customer, 114
Rich Dad Poor Dad for Teens
    (Kiyosaki and Lechter),
    81
Robinsonn, Ken, 24
Rustrum, Chelsea, 51, 69, 78

S
salaries. *See* wages
sales pitch, 108–109
sales tax, 62–63
savings account, 16, 70, 127
SBA. *See* Small Business
    Association
scheduling. *See* time
    management
School Me, 88, 109, 146
Score.org, 28, 36, 51
search engine optimization
    (SEO), 106, 108
selling your company,
    147–149
skills
    combining, 35
    delegation of, 143, 144
    passion vs., 24
slang, 101, 117

Small Business Association
    (SBA), 24, 51, 81, 148,
    149
smiling, 116social networks
    entrepreneur development,
        29, 36
    etiquette, 118
    marketing using, 105, 107
    surveying through, 102
sole proprietorship, 30–31, 32,
    59
speaking, 60, 108–109, 117
staff
    boss types quiz, 92–96
    building, 88–89
    ethical treatment of, 126
    expanding with, 142
    family and friends as,
        86–88
    firing, 87
    hiring, 85–86, 142
    internet resources for
        managing, 97
    paying, 89–90, 126
    positions needed, 84–85
    scheduling, 85
start-up costs, 44, 66
stickers, 105
storefronts, virtual, 106–107
Subway, 144
success stories, 4–5, 13, 17, 25,
    34, 37, 50, 60, 69, 80, 89,
    91, 107, 116, 125, 146
support system. *See* advisors;
    family; friends; help;
    mentors
surveys, 55, 101–102, 111, 119,
    121
sustainability. See eco-
    friendly practices
swearing, 117

T

taxes, 61–63, 124, 146
TeenEntrepreneurBootcamp
    .org, 24
time management
    expansion and, 143–144
    priority lists for, 31
    sacrifices for, 14, 15
    staff scheduling, 85
    value and, 32, 76, 140
trademarks, 56, 57, 63
transactions
    feedback opportunities,
        118–119
    tracking, 117
    virtual storefront, 106–107
Treehugger.com, 137
tutoring, 21, 100, 107. *See also*
    mentors
Tutu, Desmond, 129
Twitter auto updates, 105. *See
    also* social networks

U

*Understanding and Changing
    Your Management Style*
    (Benfari), 97
unique selling points, 100
United States Department of
    Labor, 137
United States Patent and
    Trademark Office, 56,
    63

V

Van Patten, Vanessa, 55, 91,
    106, 148
Van Veen, Ricky, 13
vendors, 127, 146
Virgin companies, 129
virtual storefronts, 106–107

vision, 35, 101, 136–137
VistaPrint.com, 104, 111

W

wages, 70, 76, 89–90, 126
warranties, 67
weakness, compensating for,
    84, 143, 144
website
    development, 22, 40, 89,
        111
    domain name, securing, 58
    for marketing, 105–106
What Matters Now (Godin), 37
*What's Next: 25 Big Ideas from
    Gen-Yers Under 25*
    (Yan), 12, 37, 79, 119,
    136
word of mouth, 104, 114, 115
WordPress.com, 106, 111
work environment, 88, 126

Y

Yan, Crystal, 12, 37, 79, 119,
    136
Yelp.com, 108, 114
Young Entrepreneurs of
    America (YEA), 24
YoungEntrepreneur.com, 36
Youth.Foundationcenter.org,
    137

Z

Zoomerang.com, 111

About the Author

Kenrya Rankin is a writer and editor whose work has appeared in more than a dozen national publications, including *Reader's Digest, Black Enterprise, Glamour, Latina, ShopSmart, Redbook,* and *Shape*. She earned her bachelor of arts in journalism with a minor in business administration from Howard University, and her master of science in publishing from New York University. A lifestyle expert, she writes about everything from entrepreneurship to health, technology, politics, relationships, and education reform, and her work has been translated into 21 languages. She's proud to be from Cleveland, Ohio, and currently lives with her husband, Tahad, in the Washington, DC area.

Acknowledgments

Thanks to my father, Henry, for always telling me I could do anything, and to my husband, Tahad, for helping to make it so. Without your encouragement, I'm just a crazy person staring at a computer screen all night. This book is for all the young people in my life: Anthony, Tylijah, Amara, Destiny, Alysse, Ethan, and Carter. You're never too young to do your own thing. Let's get started!

Thanks to my ridiculously talented editor Karen who makes everything she touches shine, to Thaisa and David for their support, to the inspiring teens who shared their stories, and to the adult entrepreneurs who let me pick their brains: Dick Demenus of Tekserve, Rachel Dooley of Gemma Redux, Charlie Graham of Shop It To Me, Maureen Kelly of Tarte, Steve Odom of Gelato, Mary Ellen Sheets of Two Men and a Truck, Adam Tate of Furniture Assembly Service & More, and Gia Veglia of Whaddya Need. You rock.

Other Zest Books

Indie Girl
From Starting a Band to Launching a Fashion Company, Nine Ways to Turn Your Creative Talent Into Reality
by Arne Johnson and Karen Macklin

Sex: A Book for Teens
An Uncensored Guide to Your Body, Sex, and Safety
by Nikol Hasler

Where's My Stuff
The Ultimate Teen Organzing Guide
by Samantha Moss with Teen Organizer Lesley Schwartz

Reel Culture
50 Classic Movies You Should Know About
(So You Can Impress Your Friends)
by Mimi O'Connor

Split in Two
Keeping It Together When Your Parents Live Apart
by Karen Buscemi

The Dictionary of High School B.S.
From Acne to Varsity, All the Funny, Lame, and Annoying Aspects of High School Life
by Lois Beckwith (aka Mimi O'Connor)

On the Bus and On the Record
22 Candid Interviews by the Teen Journalists of The Rock Star Stories
by Amanda, Brittany, Jaime, and Zac Rich
with rock journalist Aaron Burgess